Arab Spring
Women's Nightmare

Author: Shabbir H M Tankiwala

Chapter 1

What gives us value? Contemporary society would point to one of three things: appearance, accomplishments, acquisition. How you look, what you have done, what you own? As a result, women are valued on the basis of their appearance, their careers, their homes, and their experiences.

'Woman'- is a word that conjures up a lot of images in our minds and brings out varied emotions as selfless love, nurturing and caring attitude. Who is a woman? The dictionary meaning of a woman is adult female human but this definition cannot do justice to the role of woman. A woman is much more than these words.

A woman is a full circle. Within her is the power to create, nurture and transform. Understanding a woman is a mystery and it needs lots of perseverance and knowledge. A woman is the epitome of love, sacrifice, care and ability to nurture life.

Article title "**Woman and Her Significance in the Universe(10)**" commented: "Woman is first created by man's will, he dominates her and changes her whole being (hypnotism). Here is the explanation of the relation of the psychical to the physical in man and woman. Man assumes a reciprocal action of body and mind, in the sense rather that the dominant mind creates the body, than that the mind merely projects itself on phenomena, whilst the woman accepts both mental and psychical phenomena empirically. Man not only forms himself, but woman also a far easier matter.

In order to perceive and apperceive the special form, matter must not itself be formless, woman's relation to man, however, is nothing but that of matter to form, and her comprehension of him nothing but willingness to be as much formed as possible by him, the instinct of those without existence for existence. Furthermore, this "comprehension" is not theoretical, it is not sympathetic, it is only a desire to be sympathetic; it is importunate and egoistical."

The quality of a woman can be understood with these thoughts "If a woman has to choose between catching a fly ball and saving an infant's life, she will choose to save the infant's life without even considering there are men at the base." Such is the power of a woman.

Women down the ages were not given their due respects yet they went on without complaints. Women since time immemorial had powers to bring a change. Women fought with all odds to emerge as a winner.

Women now are more empowered and aware of their rights and the society has accepted their stand. The society is changing and paving way for the growth of the women. The changes can be seen in the fields of education, healthcare, equality and job opportunity. The new decade has seen a marked change in attitude towards women at large. Women have made strides in every field like politics, space exploration.

Differentiate the Male & woman "gender."

Men and women differ in their energy levels.

Men are created with an abundance of untamed energy, and this energy must be channelled or contained. Left unguided, men (and their impulses) often wreak havoc. This is the reason for much of the aggressive, violent, and dominant nature so natural to men.

The man's mind runs wild, his heart beats in a beastly fashion, and he gravitates towards forceful sports/activities. There is an obvious energy overdose.

Women, on the other hand, are created with a perfect balance of energy, and this energy must be nurtured and preserved. On their own and intuitively, women are more sensitive, subdued, and at ease.

The woman's mind thinks practically, her heart beats with compassion, and she seeks serene and productive hobbies/activities. There is an evident energy and matter of harmony.

It is quite erroneous to suppose that woman has an innate capacity to understand the individuality of a man. The lover, who is so easily fooled by the unconscious simulation of a deeper comprehension on the part of his sweetheart, may believe that he understands himself through a girl, but those who are less easily satisfied cannot help seeing that women only possess a sense of the fact not of the individuality of the soul, only for the formal general fact, not for the differentiation of the personality.

The supreme moment in a woman's life, when her original nature, her natural desire manifests itself, is that in which her own sexual union takes place. She embraces the man passionately and presses him to her; it is the greatest joy of passivity, stronger even than the contented feeling of a hypnotised person, the desire of matter which has just been formed, and wishes to keep that form for ever. That is why a woman is so grateful to her possessor, even if the gratitude is limited to the moment, as in the case of prostitutes with no memory, or, if it lasts longer, as in the case of more highly differentiated women.

Both men and women have their own unique challenges. The challenge of the man is not to let his energy run wild, and the challenge of the woman is not to let her energy run dry.

Whereas men needs to reach perfection, women needs to maintain it.

Thus, the lack of energy in hair is actually a positive expression for men but could be a negative experience for women. In women the hair contains a reduced amount of an already perfect dose of energy, thus reducing it to a dangerously low level.

Although the energy we speak of has physical manifestations and evident consequences, it is essentially a spiritual energy with much of its functionality and consequences invisible to the naked eye. And it is particularly this spirituality that we must be concerned about.

The meaning of woman is to be meaningless. She represents negation, the opposite pole from the Godhead, the other possibility of humanity. And so nothing is so despicable as a man become female, and such a person will be regarded as the supreme criminal even by himself. And so also is to be explained the deepest fear of man, the fear of the woman, which is the fear of unconsciousness, the alluring abyss of annihilation.

All the qualities of woman depend on her non-existence, on her want of character, because she has no true, permanent, but only a moral life, in her character as the advocate of pairing she furthers the sexual part of life, and is fundamentally transformed by and susceptible to the man who has a physical influence over her.

Chapter 2

"**Arab Spring Revolution**" a struggle to obtain greater freedom and desire to gain Democracy, Revolutionary movement which seemingly started in January-2011, Arabian people vociferously hit the street shouting slogans demanding civil rights and Liberties and freedom of speech, demanding more accountability, with regards to Arab spring revolution there are many pressing questions as well there are lingering doubts in mind of many of us, as in, What has it proved to be? Is it or was it a "Revolution or a Demolition"? As it is evident it has had a devastating consequences plunging entire west-Asian and north-African Islamic countries into deeper social and economic crisis and have caused unprecedented destruction. Who achieved what? Did anyone gained or did everyone lost? Was the so-called Arab spring revolution a natural born phenomenon or was it orchestrated by illuminati with sly motive to cause maximum destruction to mankind? As it is that some experts wittingly or unwittingly says "**Wars are fought for Corporate Profits,**" so with regards to

Islamic wars being fought in so many Muslim ruled countries some say it was (Arab spring revolution) a subtle start of WW3.

World economics and politics to large extent circles around Arabian and Islamic problems, problems within Islam and differences between Muslim religious and political leaders creates problems for the rest of the world, another pressing concern is the plight of women in Islam.

As the role of European powers, especially France and Britain, declined, after the two world-wars, more Arab "states" acquired independence in the 1950s and 1960s. For some years, however, violence swept through most of the newly-formed states, in the form of military coups. It was not until the late 1960s-early 1970s that the fabric of the Arab state system was more clearly defined.

The **Arab Spring** started in Tunisia in late 2010, when a self-immolation of a street vendor in a provincial town of Sidi Bouzid sparked mass anti-government protests. Unable to control the crowds, president "**Zine El Abidine Ben Ali**" was forced to flee the country in January 2011 after 23 years in power. Over the next months, Ben Ali's downfall inspired similar uprisings across the Middle East.

Throughout history, any revolution is a result of many events that completely change the nature of the society and its political life. The French revolution (1789-99), for example, was due to many factors such as economic difficulties, political rights and rising food prices.

In brief, the Arab citizen enjoyed neither liberty nor justice. Freedom, democracy and equality were foreign concepts in the conduct of governance. Up until the Arab Spring, a widely circulated proverb stated that the Arab citizens only have his/her mouth wide open at the dentist clinic. Self-expression could easily result in one's killing, imprisonment and/or forceful expulsion.

Unemployment in the Arab region is also a major source of economic insecurity and for destabilization of any political system. "Twenty-four percent of young people in the region cannot find jobs" This percentage of young unemployment is very high and the Arab countries in the region have not been able to change this situation and create new jobs, especially after the 2008 world financial crises.

The Arab Spring is a legitimate part of global civil society with moral authority and political power that does not seek to impose itself on unwilling peoples, but seeks to inspire fellow peoples under authoritarian regimes to fight for the liberties that are essential to human development and progress.

Political and human rights are fundamental for any society and Arab region lives in a situation, Even when most states arrived a very high level of democracy and political rights, the Arab region still suffers from bad political systems based on corruption, state of emergency laws, the lack of free elections and freedom of speech and religious fundamentalism, the Arabian offers a mixed bag, while its regime have remained solidly in control, Yemen's collapse has open already weak state to terrorist generation.

Poverty and poor education levels have disproportionately affected women in Egypt, affluence without legal reforms has not necessarily improved their lot in some of the wealthier Arab nations.

Women helped spark the **Arab Spring** protests in several countries and actively participated in all of them. The demonstrations were based on the issues of freedom from tyranny and patriotism, not religious ones. **Bahrain's uprising** has had some religious influence because many protesters are **Shi'ites** angry about the **Sunni** monarchy's power and discrimination against Shi'ites. However, the protests promoted democracy and the end of discrimination rather than a religious agenda. Many women's rights activists hoped the revolutions would lead to more democracy and thereby more women's rights. However, they did not explicitly push for women's rights during any of the demonstrations.

The Arab Spring is not a gender based revolution it did mark a turning point for the role of women in public space and the advent of women as part of these protests was a significant marker in the changing dynamics that were beginning to take force. The Arab Spring has been a turning point for women in the Middle East. By challenging the patriarchal norms of society, the growth of these visible women has brought about a paradigm shift in the discussion on women in the Middle East. Despite the fact that the revolutions were not gender based calls for freedom, the spotlight on women's roles across the Middle East and North Africa was intensified.

In these protests women are able to express for themselves their demands for an end to the political dictatorships, to call for the financial burdens on the countries' citizens to be lifted, to demand an end to the rising unemployment that had begun to engulf their countries. In a number of countries. **Over time, Arab societies will find a way to accommodate new expressions of Islam with democracy and women's empowerment. It's not going to be on the time schedule, however. That's the thing which really have to be understand.**

The uprising managed to undermine women's rights. Women today are exposed to abuses and atrocities. The targeting of women has become very common on towards the journey for democracy. Arab women have revolted and become outspoken lately, and they would not go back to become silent again. It is difficult to persuade the prisoner who has rebelled and broke his/her cuffs to become silent. Arab women lived for so many years on the margin, and this will not happen again. Women stand really strong by means of collective action, supporting each other and those who are blinded by lack of education and social constraints, women will be pulled backwards and it will take them too long to recover.

There are many more dynamics about the brave engagement of **women** and **men** in the Middle East who are engaging with the Arab Spring and the regional conflicts in dynamic and **creative** ways.

There is no doubt that women's rights are potentially at risk as a result of the upheaval in the Middle East. There have been **demonstrations in Egypt** calling for the instatement of Islamic law. These demands, whilst vague, could potentially have a negative effect on women's rights. In Syria, increasingly there are reports of Jihadist movements (foreign or indigenous) fighting against the regime and concern has been expressed that if they were to come to power, women's rights would be altered for the **worse**.

Islam and the veil are not the only part of the story. Whilst there have been some incredibly dispiriting stories about women's rights from **Iran** of late it should be noted that the Islamic Republic actually affords women far more rights than many other Middle Eastern states and this needs greater recognition. In Syria where the state allows women to dress as they please, society remains conservative and women's social and legal rights across ALL religions are often strictly proscribed.

As the Syrian Revolution continues, its consequences continue to affect refugees who have fled the violence in the country, especially women who are paying a double price as victims of violence in these armed conflicts.

In a patriarchal and male chauvinist culture that constantly abuses the weakness of the woman for its own interests, Syrian refugee girls in Jordan, Libya, Turkey and Lebanon are subject to the pressures of forced marriages from Syrian or other Arab nationals under the pretext of protecting their virtue at any price.

The Syrian conflict certainly has all the potential of turning into a major regional conflict between the competing forces of militant Shia and Sunni Islam. If that happens, the West will be hard-pressed to choose which side it wants to win.

Chapter 3

The Arab spring turned into Arab Nightmare: not referring simply to the tens of thousands who have been killed in Syria or in other Arabian and N-African countries, and hundreds of thousands driven away from their home into internal or external exile, the bestial barbarism into which the region has sunk.

Some political analyst have drawn comparisons between the Arab Spring movements and the **Revolutions of 1989** (also known as the "Autumn of Nations") that swept through **Eastern Europe** and the **Second World**, in terms of their scale and significance. Others, however, have pointed out that there are several key differences between the movements, such as the desired outcomes and the organizational role of **Internet** technology in the Arab revolutions.

Prominent "Sunni' Islamic extremist terrorist group "ISIS's (Islamic state of Iraq and Al-Sham) use of social media and other 21st century tools is incongruous with the material it posts on it, which often promotes a ruthless and medieval style of rule. Its members have used the platform to post gruesome pictures of the public executions and crucifixions the group has conducted in cities under their control.

What a nightmare for Syrians an other Arab countries; Civil war breaks out in your country and foreign psychopaths from across the globe come to rape, murder, torture and butcher your civilians, all in the name of Jihad (Holy War).

A small family gathering of the miniscule group of Shia Muslims in Egypt is invaded by hundreds of Sunni Muslim neighbours who bludgeon them to death, burn down their house and drag the corpse through the town.

Various Muslim clerics issues fatwa (ruling based on Islamic law) that it is all right to rape "Non-Sunni" women, whether Christian, Shia Muslim or whatever.

Demonstrators in Cairo and elsewhere gang rape a woman in full sight of all.

A rebel leader in Syria takes a bite from the Heart of a slaughter captive.

Beheading take place routinely throughout the region.

It is perfectly obvious to all but the western media and political class the "Arab Spring" has turned into a bestial nightmare.

Sad and depressing as this may sound, important to keep in mind that this situation is a consequence of human decisions, and not act of Nature or God that are beyond our capacity to repair. Decisions by Arab Men and Women has brought circumstances to this low point, better decision by Arab Men and Women can get themselves out of the pit.

Discussing Syria the most hard hit nation out of these Political Turmoil called "Arab Spring."

Syria encapsulated these ailment and distortion that have shattered the modern Arab world, including the following main ones, rampant corruption, mismanagement of socio-economic development policies, military enforced autocracy. Lack of democratic rights for citizens, non-credible and inefficient judicial systems, serious environment degradation, mediocre public education systems, weak social welfare and safety net systems, serious unchecked rural - to - urban migration, ungoverned zones of chaos within many countries, fraying borders that allows unchecked flows of people and guns, the rise of religious political fanatics, and the pervasive use of violence by all parties, including the state governments, oppositions and regional and foreign powers.

Sometimes in the 1970's the majority of Arab states left behind their Nationalist development aspiration and instead settled into a pattern of conduct that has culminated in the ghastly situation in countries like Syria and Egypt in particular, the single most debilitating reality of modern Arab history has been the Tendency for Arab countries to be ruled by single families that rely on vast security network to maintain their rule and sustain in power.

Single family rule is bad enough military-security-police states are equally bad, put them together and you get the core weakness of modern Arab state system that has seen country after country suffer the scourge of internal war, mass suffering refugee flows.

The legacy of family-military rule has included the serious of horror stories such as Muammar-Gaddafi's of Libya, Saddam Hussein in Iraq, the Assad's in Syria, Ali Abdulla Saleh in Yemen, Omar Hassan Bashir in Sudan, Zien-el-Abedine-Ben-Ali in Tunisia and the latest example Abdel Aziz Bouteflika in Algeria, The Arab monarchies have more legitimacy among their people but their societies suffer from the same underlying weaknesses and destructive tendencies that proliferate among all Arab countries.

Perplexity and despair seems to be the two sentiments that most often define people's attitudes about the mayhem in Syria, the fighting by an expanding range of Syrians, backed by a regional and global web of supporters, has reached barbaric proportion in some cases, with civilians largely paying the prices.

The number of refugees and displace people continue to grow, intense efforts to find diplomatic break-through continue through Geneva talks process, and most intervention by outside forces focus on providing humanitarian aid to the millions of Syrians in a need, wider web of Arab, Middle-Eastern and global actors pump in money and guns to keep the Syrian war going.

Women and girls have been targeted with sexual violence used to terrorize, a threat many cited as their primary reason for fleeing the country.

Young Syrian women refugees were facing the same difficulties in Turkey, including early marriages, abuse and even prostitution. There are many Syrian girls who were forced to marry older Turkish men for money. This mainly happens in families where there is no father or older brother to support them financially. Young Syrian women, therefore, were becoming the most vulnerable citizens, many of them having lost everything during the war and struggling to survive.

It has been reported by "Media" that: Scores of the Syrian women who escaped to Jordan or Lebanon out of compulsion took to prostitution, some forced or sold into it, even by their families. Some women refugees highly vulnerable to exploitation by pimps or traffickers, particularly since a significant number fled without their husbands – sometimes with their children – and had little or no source of income.

The impact of the war on neighbouring countries have kept their borders open to fleeing Syrians, even though these host countries are finding it more and more difficult to absorb any more refugees due to the pressure on their own social service infrastructure, like housing, water, education and medical-care. Though the host countries received substantial financial assistance either directly or through "united nation" and other international organization, but, still, it is below what is needed.

Perhaps one reason, why the Arab host countries, countries like Lebanon, Jordan, and Iraq keep their borders open to fleeing Syrians is that these countries have all experienced the pain of conflicts that sent many of their own citizens fleeing for shelter in neighbouring lands. So, we should keep in mind that what is happening in Syria, terrible as it is, should not be seen as an aberration in modern Arab history, but rather represents perhaps the culminating chaos of that history, Syria once referred to itself a "the throbbing heart of Arabism," that might be an appropriate description in retrospect, because the country's destruction and implosion today very much Mirror those deviant tendencies that have defined the configuration and behaviour of so many Arab countries.

Syria has in the past been known for its relatively liberal attitudes towards women, particularly in major cities such as Damascus, but the surge in Islamist groups there and the introduction of Sharia law in some regions now controlled by hard-core militants have rolled back progress in the field of gender equality. Syria's civil war has had a devastating impact on women at home and in refugee camps across borders, where they are vulnerable to trafficking, forced and child marriage and sexual violence, The Syrian woman is a weapon of war, subjected to abductions and rape by many of the militants and other groups."

Following its establishment in Syria, the Islamic State of Iraq and Al-Sham (ISIS), which has spread out over Raqqa, northern Aleppo and some of the border areas, they begun to attract young jihadists from around the world. The fighters have expropriated houses, land and cars to have the desired life in the "Islamic state." They have also married Syrian girls for various reasons. **The**

Islamic State of Iraq and al-Sham (ISIS) forces Syrian girls to marry its foreign fighters. Some parents are ready to give up everything they have to be close to the ISIS emirs (chiefs), achieve material gains and have prestige and power. They offer their daughters to foreign fighters without asking the bride-to-be, Some ISIS emirs (chiefs) marry to further integrate into Syrian society and get closer to the clans in the areas they occupy, to acquire popular support. They ask to marry a girl and her parents often have no choice but to approve, without knowing the men's history and reputation. The ISIS fighters keep their identities and histories secret, and even their names are sometimes unclear or hidden under the pretext of security, ---- according to **Media Reports**.

It gets even more complicated, Saudi Arabia and Iran are each using Syria to further their own ambitions to dominate the region. The USA is allied with Saudi Arabia but is wary that a rebel victory may not propel its interests, namely as Al Qaeda forces have gained influence in the armed opposition. Saudi Arabia and Iran are manipulating previously immaterial sectarian differences between Sunni and Shia Muslims to spur the fighting, turning a political struggle into a sectarian war. Inflaming these differences is tearing at the fabric of Syria's diverse society and may further destabilize Lebanon and Iraq as well.

Iraq was taken by surprise "when the inevitable happened" In June-2014 the Islamic radical Sunni extremist "ISIS" fully armed with combative apparatus marched inside the Iraqi territory through the Syrian border and cause havoc by capturing most of the northern Iraqi "Sunni dominated" towns and cities. A major offensive spearheaded by ISIS and also involving supporters of executed dictator Saddam Hussein overrun all of one Iraqi province and chunks of three others. When "Iraqi Government" rule over the Sunni Arab heartlands of north and central Iraq evaporated as its 300,000-strong army disintegrated. Hence, as the Iraqi army faded away in the face of Isis's offensive, the Shia as well as surprisingly even Sunni tribal fighters bravely played an increasing role in the fight-back against the Sunni militants.

The Islamic State of Iraq and the Al-Sham (Isis) massacres dozens of Iraqi soldiers in revenge for the loss of one of its commander's, hence the government supporters in Baghdad warn that the spread of fighting to the capital could provoke mass killings of the Sunni minority there, thereby plunging the country into full blown "Shia and Sunni" sectarian civil war.

What happen in Iraq now had all the makings of a civil war -- and a full-blown foreign policy crisis. Arab officials called a Sunni extremist group's military advance through Iraq a threat to Middle East security, but some in the region warned that any armed U.S. or Iranian intervention to defend the Shiite government in Baghdad could inflame Sunni Muslim anger world-wide.

The radicalization of Iraqi politics that has contributed to the current crisis in the country can be better understood with an appreciation of the role of Islamic Messianism, especially among Iraqi Shiites. This trend may even be more prominent, because if there is a battle for Baghdad, it will be fought along religious and sectarian lines.

Clearly, the crisis in Iraq began spilling far beyond its borders. Panic first gripped "Kuwait," which borders Iraq, Kuwait had to push the fellow Arab Gulf states to take a strong stand after the public release of a map attributed to the Islamic State of Iraq and al-Sham, or ISIS that showed the militant group it pushing through Kuwait's oil fields to build an Islamic caliphate across the Middle East.

Islamic state of Iraq and Al-sham (Isis) follows the gruesome extremist protocol of using the internet to publicise its atrocities, posting grisly videos of beheadings and other violence. A video purported to show the massacre of 1,700 Iraqi soldiers. The men were shot lying face down in a ditch, their hands bound behind their backs and their bodies left soaking in pools of blood. Isis has created the embryo of a Sunni Muslim caliphate straddling northern Iraq and **Syria**. With only 15,000 men, it may find it difficult to hold on to its conquests. Its base in northern Syria is like a new **Afghanistan**, a training ground and launching pad for violent extremism, just a stone's throw from Nato's southern border.

ISIS claimed to have carried out 1,000 assassinations and 4,000 bombings in Iraq in the year 2013. While fighting to overthrow Bashar al-Assad in neighbouring Syria. ISIS is believed to have a $2 billion war chest, mostly financed by rich Sunnis in **Saudi Arabia** and the Gulf sheikhdoms.

Many rich Saudis secretly thrilled by the advance of terrorist group "Isis" (Islamic state of Iraq and Al-Sham), whose atrocities are an extreme manifestation of their own Wahhabi ideology. And they will gloat mightily if ISIS fulfils its ambition of reducing every Shia shrine in Iraq to blood-spattered rubble. It is allege that "funds are being transferred from their bank accounts to the organisers of the insurgency, who despise Saudi princelings for their "Western" lifestyles but are more than happy to pocket the cash."

The recent advance made by Sunni Terrorist Group "Islamic state of Iraq and Al-Sham (ISIS)" has turned this predominantly Shi'ite country into the second battleground of a kind of Islamic Cold War. The lands of Mesopotamia, united in the shape of a state known as Iraq since 1920, now seem to be on the brink of collapse.

The Islamic Republic of Iran the main power broker in Iraq, Syria and Lebanon, insists that Iraq must be kept intact. Washington and Tehran entertain the idea of co-operating to save Iraq from ISIS, but Tehran remains deeply suspicious of US motives. "Some western powers have been claiming for years that there is a war between Sunni and Shia," By strengthening sectarian and ethnic divisions they're pursuing the dismemberment and fragmentation of the region.

There is a real danger that Islamic state of Iraq and Al-Sham (ISIS) and its allies can set up a rump state-let in northwest Iraq and northern and eastern Syria controlled by ISIS, and its allies, including groups more closely affiliated to Al Qaeda. (Al Qaeda broke with ISIS because the latter group was too willing to kill Muslims, both Sunni and Shiite.) In fact, however, ISIS can't hold Mosul for long, and it doesn't have a prayer of capturing Baghdad, nor can it get anywhere near Najaf and Karbala, the Shiite holy cities. But threats by ISIS commanders targeting those two cities are designed to inflame Shiite fears, and so they have, including in Iran, which sends countless pilgrims to Najaf and Karbala every year.

What will perhaps make the western governments and particularly the Europeans jittery is that, "Thousands" of Westerners and Americans have joined Isis, according to a top US intelligence chief, and could potentially target the "US" and other Western countries directly when they return home.

Titled *"There Is No Life Without Jihad,"* the new propaganda clip uploaded on YouTube by ISIS's Al-Hayat Media Centre allegedly shows a line-up of militants who came to Syria and later to Iraq from all over the world. The man attempts to persuade other Muslims to *"answer the call of Allah and his messenger when he calls you to what gives you life"* and join the jihad – apparently interpreting the term as armed insurgency aimed at creating an Islamic state based on Sharia law. The Islamic State of Iraq and Al-Sham (ISIS) is hoping to recruit Muslims from across the globe with the aid of YouTube, appeals from English-speaking jihadists. UK, Australian nationals are among the ISIS militants calling to support the insurgency in Iraq.

It has been reported that, Several "Dutch Muslims" inspired by jihadist movement joined the Islamic State of Iraq and al-Sham (ISIS). They discussed about Sharia, and creating an Islamic state and fighting against the Syrian regime.

ISIS has resorted to using social media to spread their message. Since the beginning of the conflict in Syria, ISIS has relied on Twitter, Instagram and Facebook to dictate their own narrative of the fighting and often to recruit other foreign fighters to join forces. "Social media is good for building a network of connections and recruitment," "Fighters talk about experiences in battle and encourage people to rise, and supporters defend and translate ISIS statements." Another example of this social media campaign emerged when a picture quickly circulated on social media showing ISIS fighters burning piles of forbidden cigarettes in Iraq. The cigarettes are considered to be "Haram" (forbidden under Islamic law) and were believed to be smuggled into the country. The picture was allegedly posted on Twitter by a Turkish jihadist.

"Jihad" attracts women as well as men. British women could be among the jihadists fighting in Syria, with around 10 predicted to have travelled to the war-torn state to join jihadist army. Hundreds of Britons are believed have gone to the country as combatants in the bloody battle against President Bashar Assad.

Ten British women were among hundreds of UK jihadists fighting a brutal holy war on the blood-soaked battlefields of Syria. Most have fled with their husbands to join the murderous faction Islamic State of Iraq and Syria, which is so vicious it has even been disowned by al-Qaeda.

After invading Iraq, The Islamic state of Iraq and Al-Sham (ISIS) fighters started ordering terrified families in Iraq to hand over their daughters for sex. Leaflets in the predominantly Sunni captured cities of Mosul and Tikrit claim the women – virgins or not – must join **Jihad**, or Holy war, and cleanse themselves by sleeping with militants. Those who refuse to do so are violating God's will, it is claimed, and will be beaten or killed. ISIS think the rape of women in this way is some kind of sexual jihad. It is not. It is a war crime, it is shame to humanity.

ISIS, in full spirit fiercely on rampage across Iraq, killing and enslaving members of the country's ancient religious minorities, including Assyrian Christians and the Yazidis.

Startling details surfaced of British female jihadists forcing captured Iraqi women into sexual slavery at brothels run by militants of the Islamic State of Iraq and Syria (ISIS), --- "British media reported." The Brothels, operated by the female "police force" called the al-Khanssaa Brigade, had been set up for the use of ISIS militants, "These women's using barbaric interpretations of the Islamic faith to justify their actions," "They believe the militants can use these women as they please as they are non-Muslims. It is the British women who have risen to the top of the Islamic State's Sharia police, and took charge of the operation," of suppressing the beleaguered Assyrian Christians and Yazidi women, the choice is either convert to Islam or face the consequence of being sexually tortured by the narcissistic Islamic militants.

ISIS chiefs have reportedly given British women such prominent roles in the ultra-religious all female militia because they see them as the most committed of the foreign female fighters. A key figure among the female police force is Aqsa Mahmood, 20 years of age with upscale academic qualification, she's from Glasgow. At least three other British females have been identified as members of the group, the Media reports suggest. 'Al-Khanssaa is a Sharia law police brigade. This is ISIS' female law enforcement," the group also include twins Salma and Zahra Halane, 16 year of age, from Manchester, and mother Khadijah Dare, 22, who is married to a Swedish militant. "It is as bizarre as it is perverse." But its barbarity against women has been treated as a side issue. Arab and Muslim governments, vocal on the threat ISIS poses to regional stability, have been virtually silent on ISIS's systemic degradation, abuse, and humiliation of women." "To the men of ISIS, women are an inferior race, to be enjoyed for sex and be discarded, or to be sold off as slaves." Young girls and women are brazenly gifted to the ISIS terrorist as reward trophy.

The effects of the Arab uprising on women are/were the starkest in Syria, where a brutal civil war has left more than 100,000 people dead and millions displaced. Moreover, the inability of the Syrian rebels, who are almost all Sunni Muslim Arabs, to win over the country's Kurds, Alawites and Christians raises the question of whether their victory is even desirable.

In the past 500 years the Middle East was part of the Ottoman Empire; the sultan ruled from afar and left non-Muslim ethnic and religious minorities pretty much alone as long as they paid their taxes – though there were many instances of massacres and forced Islamization. It all came to a sudden end after World War I. The Ottoman Empire was carved into a number of states more or less according to the whim and/or national interests of Britain and France.

The Western world—particularly the United States and the former European colonial powers—should try to understand the causes of these uprisings and carefully examine the evolution of Arab identity, particularly since the period of decolonization in the 1960s. To better understand this evolution, we need to revisit the "Arab Revolt" against Ottoman rule, which occurred from 1916 to 1918. During this time, the Arabs living in the empire understood cultural identity mainly in ethnic, not religious, terms. Pan-Arab nationalism remained the dominant paradigm in discourses about the political future of the region in 1947, when the United Nations passed the Palestine partition resolution. The paradigm thrived in the periods after the Six-Day War of 1967 and the October (or Yom Kippur) War of 1973.

Now, what happen is? That, deviating from the real purpose of seeking political freedom and power in the hands of common-man the dynamics of "Arab Spring" revolution lost its way soon and took a turn for the worse, when the jihadist minded fundamentalist forces entered the fray and sabotaged the whole revolutionary process and systematically converted the revolution into social and economic demolition by targeting various religious and ethnic minorities. The Christians, moderate Muslims, Shiites are strangled by terrorist violence in Syria, Egypt, Kenya, Pakistan. This flare up is a sign of the deep crisis of Islam, which has not yet addressed the discernment of the modern world and prefers to take refuge in an outdated Islam. The Islamic world must recognize connivance with such violence. The commitment of Christians to dialogue with Islam and modernity.

The huge changes taking place across the Middle East and North Africa, while increasing hopes for democratisation, represent for both religious and ethnic minorities perhaps the most dangerous episode since the violent break-up of the Soviet Union and the former Yugoslavia.

In Tunisia – the birthplace of the 2011 uprisings and a country that has led the way in Arab women's rights for decades – polygamy is spreading and inheritance laws are biased towards men.

The Iraqi society has suffered from policies that divided the community into males and females, until normal coexistence between genders in public places became impossible. Many Iraqis are reluctant to walk in the street with their wife or daughters or sisters, fearing that they could be harassed, while others prevent their daughters from going out from home and studying, for the same reason. There is no accurate statistics on cases of harassment, but everyone agrees that the phenomenon is increasing dramatically. Harassers escape punishment and offended women keep silent for fear of being punished, rather than seeing justice prevail.

In Palestine it is allege that many beleaguered "Jewish teenage girls from dysfunctional homes are seduced and lured into Arab villages regularly beaten and raped, often locked up with no way to escape. Mohammed calls himself Moshe, and what starts out as a search for love becomes a nightmare."

The Islamic State of Iraq and Syria (ISIS) has begun to brutally enforce Islamic laws in Mosul, Iraq, which it overran on 10-June-2014. In one instance, ISIS members entered the home of an Assyrian family in Iraqi city of Mosul and demanded the poll tax (Jizya). When the Assyrian family said they did not have the money, three ISIS members raped the mother and daughter in front of the husband and father. The husband and father was so traumatized that he committed suicide.

Heinous crime was witnessed in Egypt, when fundamentalist "Muslim Brotherhood" supporters and sympathizers went on a sexual assault and rape spree in Egypt as a way of "getting even" with those women who dared to celebrate the presidential victory of Abdel Fatteh al-Sisi—the former army chief who overthrew Muslim Brotherhood rule in Egypt. On 8-June-2014, when tens of thousands of Egyptians congregated in Cairo's Tahrir Square to celebrate Sisi's inauguration, dozens of women were sexually assaulted and many more harassed.

In **Egypt**, people's lives have been brought almost to a standstill by the breakdown of security over the past three years. Many poor women working in the informal sector who regularly buy their stock from large markets to sell on in their neighbourhoods are unable to make a living, commuting outside their immediate vicinity risks theft and abuse by thugs. When girls and women are harassed in public spaces, few dare to intervene in case the attackers are armed.

From the Atlantic Ocean to the Arabian Gulf, Arab women are humiliated. It seems that sexual harassment functions as an outlet for the repression suffered by Arab men at the hands of their politicians and for their suppressed sexual instincts.

It is through individual stories that we get an idea of how quickly things have changed. When a girl was sexually harassed in downtown Cairo in daylight in the 1990s, academics say her case was then notorious enough to provoke outrage and she became known to as the "el Ataba girl". Now reports of incidents seem to come along in their hundreds, particularly during religious festivals and political protests.

Rates of sexual harassment seem to be higher in extremely insular societies, which strictly separate the two sexes, as well as in very open societies. However, because the topic is viewed as taboo, it is shrouded in secrecy and there are not any precise statistics available. In fact, everyone seems to become angry when groups try to shed light on this dangerous phenomenon. Calls to raise awareness of the issues in the media and in schools are often frowned upon.

It cited instability and conflict in the country as well as the rise of Islamist groups in many areas as some of the reasons for that deterioration. Sexual harassment, high rates of female genital cutting and a surge in violence and Islamist feeling after the Arab Spring uprisings have made Egypt the worst country in the Arab world to be a woman, Discriminatory laws and a spike in trafficking staggering women sexual harassment statistic 99.3 percent of women and girls are subjected to sexual harassment in Egypt, which some analysts say reflects a general rise in violence in Egyptian society over the past half-decade. "There are whole villages on the outskirts of Cairo and elsewhere where the bulk of economic activity is based on trafficking in women and forced marriages."

The civil conflict had also seen government forces rape and torture women, according to rights groups, while displaced women in refugee camps are left vulnerable to trafficking, forced and child marriage and sexual violence, rampant virginity test conducted on women, Two Niqab-wearing women assaulted and forcefully cut the hair of a Christian woman on the metro Sunday.

The social acceptability of everyday sexual harassment affects every woman in Egypt regardless of age, professional or socio-economic background, marriage status, dress or behaviour.

Women who were imprisoned were threatened with sexual violence or subject to virginity tests, it has been reported that 18 female detainees were threatened with prostitution charges and forced to undergo virginity tests. They were allegedly also beaten up and given electric shocks.

If one fervently believes women should stay inside their homes and out of the business of public life, what better way to accomplish that than rampant sexual harassment and sexual assault in a country in which women's virginity and honour is the sine qua non of female participation in society?

Human Rights Watch reported that 91 women were raped or sexually assaulted in public in "Cairo's" Tahrir Square in June-2013 as protests against Mr Morsi intensified.

A dangerous increase in violence against religious minorities, especially the Coptic Christian community. As Egypt, Tunisia, and now Libya seek to construct new democratic governments, their respective approaches to religion-state issues will be critical to their success. Can these and other democratic aspirants in the region hope for stability without granting religious freedom to all their citizens? Or is the notion of religious freedom a Western concept, inapplicable to countries with different histories and cultures?

A subplot of the Arab Spring was at the beginning the endangerment of the region's Christians. How this could be connected to the people's desire to enjoy the benefits of meaningful political freedom and economic prosperity?

In the early part of the 20th century, 20 percent of the Middle East population was made-up of Christians. That number now stands at around 5 percent and is dwindling fast. The Arab Spring also has a dark under-belly. As well as ushering in nascent and fragile democracies, popular uprisings in the MENA (Middle East, North Africa) region have unleashed previously suppressed reactionary forces. The steady rise of Islamism and reactionary forces in general made life tougher for Christians and many decided to move to Christian majority countries. However, that process has been accelerated dramatically since the Arab Spring, and life for the ordinary Arab Christian in countries affected by the recent uprisings is getting worse and nightmarish. Experiencing and severely suffering more and more jihadist intimidation, sectarian strife, and political in-fighting. It has also resulted in the systematic persecution of one of the region's oldest minority communities.

Young Christian women are facing greater risk of being kidnapped by extremist, tortured, and even forced to convert to Islam since the Arab spring started in 2011. The situation for young Egyptian Christian women is uncertain, and often dire. A silent epidemic is plaguing Egypt, as young Egyptian

Christian women face abduction, torture, and rape by Muslim men. Since the Arab spring of 2011, the number of incidents have increased dramatically, with many such abductions going unreported. The horror inflicted upon the young women often includes forced conversion to Islam.

Those who live in majority Muslim nations are facing unprecedented fear and exodus as their churches and clergy are attacked. The consequences of 'majority rules' haunts the original Middle East Christians since the crucifixion itself. When Roman governor Pontius Pilate asked the assembled masses to choose between two prisoners, the majority ruled that Barabbas be released and Jesus be crucified. Despite the injustice and the manipulations, the man on the throne merely washed his hands and turned away. The besieged Christians of the Middle East fear that this history may be repeating itself.

Revolutions in the Arab world were not meant to be against the Christians or any other minority religion. The origin has never been religious, it was no more than social, economic, and civic. Afterwards Islamist movements entered and affected the presence of Christian and other minority people, but it was not the Arab revolution's purpose.

Iraq was a precursor in that it illustrated what happens in the Middle East when a tyrannical dictator is overthrown and a power vacuum is created. In Iraq we saw the emergence of Jihadism, sectarian strife, and political in-fighting: three problems that are often inter-connected and feed off one another. In Egypt, Al-Qaeda issued an open declaration of war on Egypt's Coptic Christians, Egypt's Copts are more fearful than ever. The past few years have seen a steady rise in violent attacks against "Coptic Christians" and fire-bombings of Coptic churches.

A foreign woman was allegedly stripped and sexually assaulted in Egypt's iconic Tahrir Square, it is alleged that "dozens of men surrounded her and started grabbing her," when she screamed for help some people came, but they were hit in the face," "appalling," it is learnt that "The men just started tearing at her clothes and grabbing her body all over. When she fought back, they pushed her. One can imagine "It must have been brazen and chaotic situation."

In one more such gruesome incident, A Dutch journalist was raped at Cairo's central Tahrir square by a group of Five Men, when millions of protestors had gathered demanding the ouster of the then Egypt president "Mursi," the beleaguered Dutch journalist its believed had to undergo surgeries for horrific injuries she sustained during sexual attack.

Raping foreign journalists -- guaranteed to attract global attention -- is merely a more efficient way of getting that message across.

Religious and cultural implications in regards to women complicate the issue, in the Middle East, rape is more a tool of social repression than of warfare. In these instances rape can be almost ceremonial, and has deep meaning and consequences in Islamic culture. Rape was used excessively during Muammar Gaddafi's attempt to remain in power in Libya. The case of Iman Al-Obeidi—a woman who burst into a Tripoli hotel filled with foreign journalists who then told the world she was raped by the government authorities, her revelation brought the Gaddafi regime's use of rape as a tool of political repression into the international spotlight.

In Libya there were reports of mass rape committed by government mercenaries, Gaddafi was accused of carrying out his own atrocities as doctors revealed that patients had been targeted in their beds by snipers who surrounded a hospital, killing anyone who tried to escape and firing through windows. Rebel fighters at the scene initially insisted that these Gaddafi 'rats' had been drinking whisky all day and had then gone mad under the stress of the rebel onslaught, and turned their guns on each other.

Throughout Gaddafi's fight to remain in power, his regime ordered soldiers to go into villages and rape the female adults and children, some as young as 8 years old, in front of family members. Condoms and Viagra were found in pockets of dead Gaddafi soldiers. Children described being forced to watch as their fathers were murdered and their mothers raped.

It is also worth evaluating the reaction of Muslims. In some cases, they say, this is unacceptable! But what does this mean? What is being done to stop these groups? To answer this question we need to understand where the violence comes from. In fact, it is the mental formation, the education received, which drives the terrorists to violence. Backed by a learned Imam, who emits a fatwa (legal judgment), they become accustomed to using violence against anyone who does not think like them.

Chapter 4

The Middle East is in a downward spiral. More than 160,000 have died in Syria's civil war, the Islamic State of Iraq and Syria, aka ISIS, in June-2014 captured key Iraqi cities on its march towards the Iraqi capital "Baghdad," hence the security investments made by the U.S. over the past decade—like them or not—have been frittered away.

According to Some political observers and commentators assessment of fluid political situation in Syria is: "In a systematic and organized way, the United States and some of its regional and trans-regional allies have concocted a scheme for Balkanizing Syria through embroiling the country's different religious sects in an erosive and seemingly unending clashes, Sunnis against the Alawites and Twelver Shiites against the Christians. This will ultimately result in acrimony, quarrel and bitterness in Syria and pave the way for what the enemies of peace and harmony in Syria have been looking for: the dismantlement of the government of President Bashar al-Assad. Some analysts believe that Syria is paying the price for its resistance against Israel. Of course Israel, which directly benefits from conflict and unrest in Syria, is inclined to see a chaotic, turbulent and tumultuous Syria rather than a Syria which is unified, strong and powerful. This belief that Israel sees its interest in the continuation of unrest in Syria is substantiated by many analysts and politicians who have closely monitored the developments in the Middle East in the recent years."

I discovered some startling facts in an article that I read about the potential causes that may have spark the political crisis called "Arab Spring," in an, Article title, **"ISIS "Made in USA". Iraq "Geopolitical Arsonists" Seek to Burn Region,"** which stated that: "The Islamic State of Iraq and Al-Sham

(Syria) (ISIS) is a creation of the United States and its Persian Gulf allies, namely Saudi Arabia, Qatar, and recently added to the list, Kuwait. The Daily Beast in an article titled, "America's Allies Are Funding ISIS," states:

The Islamic State of Iraq and Syria (ISIS), now threatening Baghdad, was funded for years by wealthy donors in Kuwait, Qatar, and Saudi Arabia, three U.S. allies that have dual agendas in the war on terror.

Despite the candour of the opening sentence, the article would unravel into a myriad of lies laid to obfuscate America's role in the creation of ISIS. The article would claim:

The extremist group that is threatening the existence of the Iraqi state was built and grown for years with the help of elite donors from American supposed allies in the Persian Gulf region. There, the threat of Iran, Assad, and the Sunni-Shiite sectarian war trumps the U.S. goal of stability and moderation in the region.

However, the US goal in the region was never "stability" and surely not "moderation." As early as 2007, sources within the Pentagon and across the US intelligence community revealed a conspiracy to drown the Middle East in sectarian war, and to do so by arming and funding extremist groups including the Muslim Brotherhood and Al Qaeda itself. Published in 2007 – a full 4 years before the 2011 "Arab Spring" would begin – Pulitzer Prize-winning journalist Seymour Hersh's New Yorker article titled, ""The Redirection: Is the Administration's new policy benefiting our enemies in the war on terrorism?" stated specifically (emphasis added):

To undermine Iran, which is predominantly Shiite, the Bush Administration has decided, in effect, to reconfigure its priorities in the Middle East. In Lebanon, the Administration has cooperated with Saudi Arabia's government, which is Sunni, in clandestine operations that are intended to weaken Hezbollah, the Shiite organization that is backed by Iran. **The U.S. has also taken part in clandestine operations aimed at Iran and its ally Syria. A by-product of these activities has been the bolstering of Sunni extremist groups that espouse a militant vision of Islam and are hostile to America and sympathetic to Al Qaeda.**" ("So after reading this article, it seems that "there's more to it than meets the eyes," perhaps maybe "Arab Spring" was not a sporadic revolutionary struggle that began from "Tunisia" but well plotted and thought off and deliberately created political crisis.")

To understand and to have broader perspective of this so-called Arab spring revolution – that has turned into Arabian nightmare and has sparked brutal sectarian conflict, internal rift and differences within Islam has profoundly succeeded in destabilising entire Islamic world, Sunni-Muslim jihadists involve in frequent terrorist attacks targeting western countries and ruthlessly killing non-Muslim people throughout the world has stigmatize entire world's Muslim population, **is it the start of World War 3?** Are the **Illuminati** who allegedly orchestrated World War II, are they back in game and have succeeded in starting WW3?

Have a listen to another view point; Article in **"What is the New World order?"** Describes astounding motives: "The term **New World Order (NWO)** has been used by numerous politicians **through the ages**, and is a generic term used to refer to a worldwide conspiracy being orchestrated by an extremely powerful and influential group of genetically-related individuals (at least at the highest echelons) which include many of the world's wealthiest people, top political leaders, and corporate elite, as well as members of the so-called **Black Nobility** of Europe (dominated by the **British Crown)** whose goal is to create a **One World (fascist) Government**, stripped of nationalistic and regional boundaries, that is obedient to their agenda.

Listen to the Zionist* banker, Paul Warburg:

"We will have a world government whether you like it or not. The only question is whether that government will be achieved by conquest or consent." (February 17, 1950, as he testified before the US Senate).

Their intention is to effect **complete and total control** over every human being on the planet and to dramatically reduce the world's population by two thirds. While the name *New World Order* is the term most frequently used today to loosely refer to anyone involved in this conspiracy, the study of exactly who makes up this group is a complex and intricate one.

Why the Conspiracy is Unknown?

The sheer magnitude and complex web of deceit surrounding the individuals and organizations involved in this conspiracy is mind boggling, even for the most astute among us. Most people react with disbelief and scepticism towards the topic, unaware that they have been **conditioned** (brainwashed) to react with scepticism by institutional and media influences. Author and de-programmer Fritz Springmeier (*The Top 13 Illuminati Bloodlines*) says that most people have built in "slides" that short circuit the mind's critical examination process when it comes to certain sensitive topics. "Slides", Springmeier reports, is a CIA term for a conditioned type of response which dead ends a person's thinking and terminates debate or examination of the topic at hand. For example, the mention of the word "conspiracy" often solicits a slide response with many people."------

The bloodletting and violence in Syria has caused sectarian conflict, it can be maintained that the years of civil war in Syria has very bold sectarian overtones and many of the motivations of the parties involved in the war are sectarian. Unquestionably, one is that the Takfiris and Salafists in Syria are dismayed that the Sunni majority country is being ruled by a Shiite Alawite government, and their consternation has gone to such extremes that they have taken up arms against the government, brutally behead its supporters and kill whoever they think is somewhat related to or supportive of the government.

It's understandable that Americans are sick and tired of being involved in Middle East conflict and want to finally stay neutral, but for it to decide when to get the break. Even if USA didn't get involved, US would have many of the economic problems everyone is complaining about for a while, and entering Syria isn't going to make USA's debt skyrocket. Plus, for those paranoid about a WWIII, the chances of it are very unlikely, because no countries are siding with Syria. Russia did not state that it will defend Syria and actually admitted that there is a chance it will support the U.N. Action if it is without doubt that al-Assad truly used chemical weapons. What are "USA" going to lose if it joins? Unfortunately, they will put more lives at risk, initially, but in the end far more will be lost if the "USA" stand by like cowards and say "there's nothing we can do about it" when it could have at least tried.

America has suffered greatly from the abuse of presidential war powers and lost much blood and treasure because of the unitary theory of the executive, which views the President as a sovereign and not one among equals, as the founders envisioned.

U.S. involvement would likely had been used as a recruitment tool for extremists on both sides of the fight in Syria. And the very allies who are claiming USA must act to protect could find themselves square in the centre of a target. A limited strike on Syria could result in a retaliatory chemical weapons attack on Israel if Assad actually carried out the initial chemical strike.

An American military attack against Assad will strengthen the hand of those who seek to turn Syria into an Islamic state. And if that happens, neighbouring Jordan will almost certainly fall to a **jihadist movement**. The tumbling of those dominoes as a result of an ill-conceived U.S. intervention in Syria's civil war would also bring down Iraq's government. Nearly **4,500 American** servicemen and women died to create a democracy in that Middle Eastern country, which is wedged between Iran, Syria and Jordan. But that fledgling government might not survive if it is surrounded by militant Islamic states.

In Syria's civil war, there is no moral high ground. There is only the quicksand of a wider Middle East conflict that the U.S. must carefully navigate. **While the implacable and oppressive actions of the Assad regime, which include the senseless murder of civilians and suspected deployment of chemical weapons, seem to provide sufficient reason for the U.S. to intervene, there are myriad reasons why doing so would be in direct conflict with American interests and only serve to amplify the chaos.**

The Arab people were not ready to embrace democracies like western civilizations. It was a clash of cultures like the Crusades a millennium ago. Suddenly, a political tsunami, known as the Arab Spring, swept away rulers in Tunisia, Algeria, Libya, Egypt and Yemen. It threatens next to topple Assad in Syria and may yet undermine the Islamic regime in Iran.

Americans have had enough and, significantly, They especially are dumfounded by women who vote to legalize polygamy and agree to wear the burka. The American people are through with intimate ties to the Muslim Middle East. They are ready for the American Winter.

The mandate given by people of "US" in 2008 presidential election to "**Barak Obama**" was too not to involve "United States of America" militarily in any more wars overseas. The people of America had seen enough of blood of their soldiers fighting wars and war on terror on overseas soil, hence, President Barak Obama respecting the overwhelming opinion and desire of the people of "U.S." honouring the mandate he was given by the people of "U.S.A," President Obama wisely restrain himself from any kind of overt interference in the Arab spring revolution struggle. Also to dislodging a secular and liberal President Like Syria's "**Bashar-Al-Assad**" from power, would have been counter-productive for U.S. government because abrupt ouster of Assad could potentially had destabilized entire Arabian region which would had proved disastrous not only for Americans but for many other Islamic countries.

Also with regards to Syria, many political observers have failed to take note of prevailing ground reality, which is that Syrian population consist of well over dozen plus "religious and ethnic communities," the fact is that "Sunni Muslims" maybe the large majority community and apparently which also is the only religious community that is hell-bent on getting rid of the incumbent Syrian president "Bashar-Al-Assad" out of power from Syria's president-ship, but except for the large chunk of Sunni Muslim group, all the remaining "religious and ethnic communities" be it the "Shia's or its offshoots communities like the "Alawites, Druze, or the Ismailis, than other ethnic communities like Kurds or the Christians, Jews and many other communities" all these "Non-Sunnis" religious and ethnic communities are steadfast and overwhelmingly supports and favours the continuance "Bashar-Al-Assad" as the president of Syria. Hence it becomes mandatory duty of Syrian President Assad to save the sovereignty of his country "Syria" and fight the insurgent Sunni Islamic extremist terrorists that has infiltrated inside Syria and is causing havoc in civil societies and forcing its hard-line draconian chemistry on civil population of Syria. If America can attack and wage war on countries like Afghanistan and Iraq on the pretext of safeguarding its sovereignty and on pretext of "War on Terror" America can launch "Drone" strikes in countries like "Pakistan, Yemen, Somalia etc, so, why not? Syrian President Bashar-Al-Assad being commander in chief of Syrian army order his forces to attack the Jihadis and destroy terrorists camps and bases inside Syria. The Sunni extremist terrorists who have entered inside Syria, there darkest desire and motive is to destroy Syria and impose abrasive "Sharia Law."

But, overall, at least the people of America will welcome a reprieve from the focus and expenditure of time and treasure on that part of the world. It will be good to take a break for a decade or two. It will be healthy for Americans to allow the Middle East to straighten out its own house.

The overthrow of repressive regimes has paved the way for Islamists to occupy the political landscape. They believe this might enable Islamists to threaten individual rights, culture, arts, and the very notion of democracy itself. Thus, there are some who believe the uprisings against Arab regimes have lead to the worst possible scenario since those regimes were able to guarantee limited margins of freedom by ruling out the threat of Islamists.

The sad truth is that the dominant Western policy towards the Arab people traditionally has been one of containment. Today many applaud as the people of the region take to the streets to claim their rights, but until recently Western governments frequently acted as if the Arab people were to be feared, hemmed in controlled. The Arab Spring showed that many people in the region do not share the West's comfortable complacency with autocratic rule. No longer willing to be the passive subjects of self-serving rulers, they began to insist on becoming full citizens of their countries, the proper agents of their fate.

Article title; **Avoid a classic blunder: stay out of religion wars in the Middle East**: "Muslims in the Middle East are fighting wars of religion. Like the carnage between Protestants and Catholics that haunted Northern Ireland during the last third of the 20th century, there is little anyone can do until local peoples crave peace so intensely they are willing to cultivate it. History shows that outside meddling only intensifies sectarian fury. Stopping internecine war begins at home. President Barack Obama imperils Americans by trying to excise an abscess that can be cured only from the inside out. The decision to re-engage in Iraq, and the wider Middle East, also contradicts the president's other, bigger objective: to exit the nanny business. The last time religious aggression swept an entire subcontinent was during the Reformation four centuries ago, when Christians hashed out their hatreds much as Muslims of the Middle East are doing today. Islamic State (ISIS), or as the President Obama calls it, the Islamic State in Iraq and the Levant, is fighting to restore a caliphate. Catholics and Protestants spent decades warring over similar issues. Should all Christians accept the same religious doctrine? Should all nations be under the dominion of the pope?

The first Islamic Civil War, from 656 to 661, created two competitive sects – Sunni and Shi'ite. Neither recognized the other's legitimacy.

Sunnis bowed to a caliph who ruled over all believers regardless of nationality. The last caliph was Sultan Abdülmecid II. Kemal Ataturk, the resolute builder of modern Turkey, fired Abdülmecid in 1924. The 400-year-old caliphate in Istanbul vanished. Unsurprisingly, not everyone was happy about the rupture. In 1928, the Muslim Brotherhood began in Egypt. That group and other like-minded sectarian organizations gradually spread into the new secular nations of Syria, Jordan, Iraq and Iran." ------Elizabeth Cobbs Hoffman. --------

On the larger geopolitical level, meanwhile, one thing appears to be certain: the west will have less impact in shaping the Arab world's future than in decades past. The reasons for this are varied: they include the more complex internal politics of western states, which have been badly affected both by the economic and financial crisis since 2008 and by the costly, inconclusive wars in Afghanistan and Iraq. These factors have resulted in greater caution about foreign-policy entanglements, and this in turn reinforces ongoing changes in the geo-economic balance of power worldwide. In this fluid situation, neither regional powers nor global institutions appear ready on their own to fill gaps in authority or provide new direction.

Decades after emancipation from colonial rule, the quest for independence still figures highly on the Arab agenda, and in this quest the pursuit of authenticity has moved to centre stage. Authenticity represents, of course, a highly complex concept, more complex at any rate than many of its partisans would have their audiences believe. While some debate the relative weight of Arabism versus local attachments (Egyptian identity, Iraqi nationalism), Islamist activists have a simple answer: Authenticity is identical with Islam -- not the Islam actually practiced by the so-called popular masses, an Islam already corrupted by misconceptions, magic and superstition, but the true Islam of the age of the Prophet and his Companions, or rather their image of that true Islam. This Islam, so they claim, is the solution to all problems of private and public life, of state and society, the yardstick by which to measure values, goals and institutions. Western techniques and modes of organization may be acceptable, but there is a strict refusal to adopt un-Islamic values. The distinction at once complicates the matter, for liberal democracy clearly involves both techniques and values.

Because it is associated with Western modes of thinking and behaviour, liberal democracy is always in danger of being associated with Western misdeeds, real and alleged. To many Arabs and Muslims, Western economic, political and cultural influence appears more pernicious than ever. The so-called intellectual onslaught (Al-Ghazw al-Fikri) on Arab-Islamic culture and identity is a main theme of the day, and many see liberal democracy as part of that assault. Its advocates risk being charged with cultural mimicry, importing non-Islamic, unauthentic models of thought and organization. Hence the necessity either to authenticate liberal and democratic notions, structures and procedures by establishing their Islamic pedigree, or else to prove that Arab-Islamic tradition is in fact superior to Western liberal democracy, on a moral as well as a practical level. This accounts for much of the uneasy, if not distorted, character of the debate, its accusations, apologetics and mutual recrimination.

The advent of saviours is one of the salient features of all Abrahamic religions, and is an idea that manifested itself differently in all three of those religions: Judaism, Christianity and Islam. This idea grows and evolves throughout history, usually as a result of harsh social and political circumstances that drove people into seeking divine intervention from a heavenly emissary that would restore the tide of history back on to the righteous path.

Despite the challenges it has brought, the experience being suffered by the people of Syria today and the economic and social problems that many of these countries are now grappling with, the Arab Spring holds greatest prospect for the enlargement of greater freedom and dignity since the end of the Cold War.

What's the reason behind Shia and Sunni conflict? Why so much bitterness between these two rival Islam faction? Ever since the death of Prophet Mohammed in 632 A.D, after the death of Prophet "Islam" was divided into two factions, the Shia's followed "**Imam Ali**" the prophet's son-in-law, to whom the Prophet Muhammed had in his life time had in a public ceremony at a place called "**Ghadir Khumm"** (now in Saudi Arabia) declared his "Heir," but, the Sunni's did a volte-face after the Prophet's death and they refused to accept "Imam Ali as their leader and instead they selected their own leader as "Caliph," hence Islam split into two faction the "Shia's and Sunni's," Ever since division in Islam the Sunni-Muslims have severely harmed, humiliated and mercilessly been killing the Shia faction of Islam, the Shia Islamic community is arguably the most suppressed and oppressed community in the world.

There is a Distinct Dissimilarities between the two rival Islamic faction of the "Shia's and Sunni's."

The records are there to speak for themselves, pick up any Islamic history books and you'll find that: The Shia Islam's entire religious hierarchy all their Imams (chief religious priests) have proved to be an ideal example of "Extreme Tolerance and Supreme Sacrificial."

While The Sunni Muslim Sect has history of indulging in violence and are extremely intolerant towards every other religion and they have been profoundly practicing hatred and violence as a tool to become a supreme and overriding power.

Also it will be worth noting that all the monstrous Islamic jihadi (Islamic holy warrior) terrorist groups like "Al-Shabaab, Al-Qaeda, Al-Nusra, Boko-Haram, Taliban, Islamic state for Iraq and Al-Sham (ISIS) etc," are all diehard followers of Sunni Islam.

Islam-phobia: why other religions fear and dislikes Islam? Or, does religions help us human at all? Let's understand.

Karl Marx saw religion as a political tool utilized by the oppressing ruling classes, arguing that it is in the interest of the ruling classes to instil in the masses the religious conviction that their current suffering will lead to eventual happiness, so that they will not attempt to make any genuine effort to understand and overcome the real source of their sufferings. It was on this basis that he described religion as "the opium of the people."

The problem is when you mix civilized 21st century culture, with cultures that are still based on ancient believes and following the laws and tradition of yesteryears. The yeast of barbarity rises and the flames of cruelty burn deeply, all compassion is thrown to the winds.

The facts show a clarity that human kind cannot live in harmony due to indoctrinations that have been passed on from generation to generation. With that indoctrination, hatred and religious based vendettas of our ancient past have infected human society with distrust and jealousy of others that follow different Gods.

It can also be argued that religions do tremendous harm to society through their use of war, violence and terrorism to promote their religious goals. Religious leaders often contribute to secular wars and terrorism by endorsing or supporting the violence, and conversely, religious fervour is often exploited by secular leaders to support war and terrorism. In a world largely dominated by the religious moralities of various factions, we are still constantly beset by wars, injustice and brutality.

The evidence from the database largely discredits the common wisdom that the personality of suicide bombers and their religion are the principal cause of their actions. It shows that though religion can play a vital role in the recruitment and motivation of potential future suicide bombers, their real driving force is a cocktail of motivations including politics, humiliation, revenge, retaliation and altruism. The configuration of these motivations is related to the specific circumstances of the political conflict behind the rise of suicide attacks in different countries. "Religion is not THE problem," "But it then becomes problematic because religion brings a whole host of absolutistic symbols and images and justifications" that act as an accelerant to terrorism.

Why Religious Militants Kill," has come at it in a different way, for many Muslim youths, the idea of terrorism under the guise of "jihad" became a "global fad" akin to gangsta rap. In short, it's less a religious phenomenon than "a cool way of expressing dissatisfaction with a power elite." "Jihad has become a millenarian movement with mass appeal, similar, in many ways, to earlier global movements such as the anarchists of the 19th century or even the peace movement of the 1960s and '70s," radical youth are expressing their dissatisfaction with the status quo by making war, not love.

Islam-phobia has come to be interpreted by many as the irrational fear of Islam or Muslims. The problem arises when its main use is to describe people with quite rational fears. The problem with the term 'Islam-phobia' is that due to the illogical use to which it has been put, it has managed to elude proper definition. Furthermore, pro-sharia activists and sympathisers prefer to keep the term as nebulous as possible since this assists their agenda. If a rational definition is created then it is more difficult for the term to be used as a tool stifle debate and demonise people.

History is behind some of the radical Muslim hatred of the "west" but so are cultural difference. A westerner, an American, a non-Muslim, or a Muslim of a different stripe than they, then some radical Muslims hate you, why? The answer is complex and involves history, culture, politics, religion and psychology. The belief that Islam as politically manifest and capable of determining actual laws promotes inequality, injustice, and moral incorrectness. Many non-Muslims are Anti-Islamic and point to a number of issues with Islamic legal practice and belief. Some of these Islamic "ideas" are incredibly frightening to many non-Muslims. The discussions about declaring Holy Wars on Unbelievers, are very frightening and scary to many who treasure the idea of Freedom of Conscience. Furthermore, Islam as a religion may promote tolerance of other religions, but certainly does not promote equality between religions.

Furthermore frightening: Islamic Penal Law makes Non-Muslims very scared. Some particularly problematic issues includes: claiming that the rape victim is criminally liable for "getting raped," chopping off a thief's hands as punishment for theft, the execution of homosexuals, blasphemy laws in general, permission given to enslave people, and execution of apostates.

Boston bombing as an example of what happens when Islam-phobia as the irrational fear of questioning Islam is not taken into consideration by policy makers who often appear to be its most acute sufferers. Islamophobia lacks some of the traditional elements of religious persecution, the subtle hostility against Muslims could escalate to overt attacks, there's no sign that violence against Muslims is on the rise, for instance — there's plenty of anecdotal evidence that hate speech against Muslims and Islam is growing both more widespread and more heated."

Islam phobia is one of the overriding factors behind the policy of persecution and oppression of the Muslims by the "US" and its non-Muslim allies. Muslim-Christian antagonism dates back to the period of "Prophet Muhammad" who was blessed with prophet hood in 610AD. In less than twenty years he transformed the savage Arab tribes into a civilized people. When Mecca was captured in 630AD and cleared of all the idols.

The practice of only welcoming select members of a marginalized identity, particularly those who have acclimated to the dominant group. Racists occasionally celebrate people of colour who have gravitated away from their identity and toward the white majority, just as Islamophobes occasionally celebrate ex-Muslims who have cast aside their supposedly harmful beliefs.

Islam is a religion, and while one can attack ideas, one must not attack religions. It is, however, quite insulting for religions to deny that they are ideas. Religions are certainly more than ideas, they are theological belief systems, but they are also ideas about how society should be run just as much as liberalism and conservatism are. Therefore, Islam, or Christianity, or Judaism, or Buddhism should be just as subject to criticism as conservatism or liberalism.

The disadvantaged position of Muslim minorities, evidence of a rise in Islamophobia and concern over processes of alienation and radicalisation have triggered an intense debate in the European Union regarding the need for examining community cohesion and integration policies. Islamophobia and anti-Muslim racism causes victims to adhere more strongly to Islam as a part of self-identity. It leads to Muslims seeking out and learning from Islamic outreaches that present a stronger and more dominant image of Islam, such as those from Islamic countries, and therefore works against integration with the West.

The thing that uniquely defines religion, the thing that sets it apart from every other ideology or hypothesis or social network, is the belief in unverifiable supernatural entities. Of course it has other elements - community, charity, philosophy, inspiration for art, etc. But those things exist in the secular world, too. They're not specific to religion. The thing that uniquely defines religion is belief in supernatural entities. Without that belief, it's not religion. And with that belief, the capacity for religion to do harm gets cranked up to an alarmingly high level - because there's no reality check.

Religion is not the only belief that inspires good people to do evil things. Political ideology can do all that quite nicely. People have committed horrors to perpetuate Communism, an ideology many of those people sincerely believed was best. But horrors have been committed in the name of democracy and freedom, as well.

Chapter 5

Social inequality and discrimination against women.

What about the Burqua's Muslim women are forced to wear? The systematic executions of innocent Christian women for witchcraft in the Middle-Ages? The barring of women becoming Catholic priests? The polygamous lifestyle of Mormons? The "honour" executions of Muslim wives for any infraction to the patriarchal interpretation of the Quran? The horrific mutilations of female genitals practiced by religious figures in Central Africa and Middle East? It seems every world religion is intensely patriarchal. Every one of them engages in the systematic devaluation of women, in the systematic exclusion of women from positions of authority, and in the systematic oppression and even enslavement of women. I have yet to find a single major religion that bucks this trend. Considering how little many of these religions have in common otherwise, this is a truly remarkable pattern.

Repression and exploitation are different, but complementary, forms of control and abuse of female sexuality. Women and girls' sexuality is repressed by strict control on sexual activity through such customs as placing a premium on girls' virginity, basing family honour on the sexual control of daughters and wives, exacting severe punishment for adultery, preventing equal access to divorce, and segregating girls and women from boys and men. Patriarchal religions, which mould most of the cultures of the world, subordinate women and girls to men. Fundamentalist movements, whether Christian, Jewish, Hindu or Islamic, advocate the repression of women and girls' sexuality. Women and girls' interaction with men and boys is closely monitored and restricted and their bodies and hair covered in a way deemed to be modest. For example, under the influence of Islamic fundamentalism, women are required to wear full body coverings, such as chadors and Burqas. Punishment for sexual misconduct can be severe, as in Iran, where women can be legally stoned to death.

Female abuse is a common phenomenon that takes shape in several forms in societies. However this phenomenon tends to be extreme in certain communities, where women are mercilessly "Battered" by males of their household.

The magnitude of the problem of the Battered women is not only the result of the damage these women go through during and after being battered, but also the result of secrecy that they are forced to keep out of fear that if they divulge their sufferings they will bring dishonour to themselves and their families.

Definition of honour killing is when a family member, or clan member, takes the life of another family member (who has shamed the family) in order to restore honour to the family or clan. Both men and women are victims of honour killing, however, women tend to be the victim more often and it is common for younger brothers to commit the murder. These crimes happen because of cultural behaviour and how that society views acceptable and unacceptable behaviour. It is supported by fundamentalist who are in governing roles. There are no laws to protect the women. There are expectations within society that forces citizens to continue these crimes. If one attempts to challenge these practices, they will die.

The reasons that stand behind women "Battering" are many, some men beat women because they feel physically strong. Ironically this physical superiority is only displayed over females, almost never over other "Males."

Its widely perceived and believed that there is no document in the world that states that the "Male" is in anyway better than female, and such behaviour only reveals perverted traditions and Male insecurity.

The vulnerability of Muslim women as a whole. Time and again, verbal and physical attacks on Muslim women increases when they have these so-called national debates. In emotional and psychological terms. Women who wear the veil "are trying to observe what they feel are their religious convictions," If a woman is, in fact, being oppressed into covering up, then enforcing a stance which makes it difficult or impossible for her to move about in public it cuts off her chances of finding any support outside the home.

Talk to any Arab women and you'll quickly learn that the controversy over Muslim "Veil" that rages endlessly. The Arab women face daunting array of hardship from spousal domination at home to gender discrimination in the work place, and if they happen to agree that the Veil symbolizes their plight, they tend to dismiss criticism of it as a western attack on their culture.

The topic of women right in the Arab world can be as confusing as it is culturally explosive. The Arab conspiracy theory that promoting women's right is part of a western plot against Islam.

The advancement of women has long been an Arab goal. In Egypt women's right organization was founded in 1881, Arab world and its achievement of human development.

Although Arab girls who attend school outperform the boys, yet the Arab girls generally have fewer educational opportunities. The Arab countries collectively have one of the highest rates of female illiteracy in the world. Lack of education as well as gender discrimination combine to keep the percentage of employed Arab women at only One-third, the lowest in the world.

These significantly contributes to unhealthy lifestyles, resulting in the highest rate of disease and deaths linked to pregnancy and child-birth.

Arab women largely excluded from political participation, Apart handful of few Arab women cabinet ministers tend to hold symbolic rather than influential positions.

The Arab women often suffer domestic violence, including so-called "honour killing," behind a societal cloak of silence. Stricter Islamic law implemented in most Arab countries restrict women's personal liberties, for example by giving them lesser status than husbands in divorce proceedings and requiring the permission of a husband or father to work, travel or borrow from a bank.

Often, women's issues are trivialised into whether or not to wear the veil or shake hands with men outside their family, and while larger issues, such as domestic violence, are being the central issue of what "equality" means and how it is expressed go largely ignored. For example, domestic violence is wrong because it creates pain and suffering and is unjust, but the central belief of a man's right to rule over his wife is not always part of this discussion.

The predicament of Arab women is the region longstanding patriarchal tradition of protection and "honour" wrapped into tribal identity. The Authoritarian regimes that emerged with Arab independence a half century ago have undermine the liberal institution and values that might have better encouraged women's rights and protected under a rule of law.

In some Muslim circles, the "F" word (feminism) raises as many tensions as eyebrows, immediately conjuring images of the dominating, angry, family-hating woman. But like other images that comes to mind upon mention of any label, including the image of the oppressed woman that often comes to mind when one hears "Muslim," this gut reaction is based on stereotypes that may be true in a very specific historical and social context, but does not hold water when compared to a larger reality, and therefore does not justify the hostility that follows. Important distinction. "Islamic feminism" is not simply a feminism that is born from Muslim cultures, but one that engages Islamic theology through the text and canonical traditions.

Women's prospects are further weakened by regressive Islamic jurisprudence that effectively codifies discrimination against women, so entrenched has this discrimination become, In Saudi Arabia women banned in the country from driving, denied the right to travel without the permission of their male 'guardian,' or husband's consent and required to wear a veil from head to toe, are now to be monitored by a new electronic system that tracks cross-border movement. Saudi Arabia is the only country in the world where women are not allowed to drive. In Saudi Arabia, there have long been a group of elite women who have been able to work in specific jobs - as doctors or teachers. But retail was closed off to them, until a 2011 decree from King Abdullah, allowing women to work in Lingerie Shops.

Despite gloomy picture of current states of affair, many brave Arab women and their male supporters to remedy the situation and the gains they have made.

According to the No More Abuse site, "The phenomenon of battered women in Saudi Arabia is much greater than is apparent on the surface," it says. "It is a phenomenon found in the dark. We want to achieve justice for all women and children exposed to abuse in all parts of the Kingdom." It's a watershed moment for the nation, which is known for its gender inequalities. According to Human Rights Watch, women in Saudi Arabia are still treated as minors under the guardianship system, which requires them to receive permission from their husbands, brothers or fathers in order to travel, study or work. Rates of abuse are difficult to determine in the country, because much like the U.S. or other countries, domestic violence often goes unreported.

The sundry array of "Islamic feminisms" throughout the Muslim world. Women in all these contexts are encountering the tradition based on their respective cultures, needs, priorities, and resources, creating a well-rounded picture of a global movement in which women create their own path to knowledge and move forward with it. In some contexts, this means addressing fundamental rights such as freedom from violence, while in others women carve out their own space and find room to challenge traditional dogma, rediscovering Islam's feminine history and room for future discourse.

There is a large disconnect between religious feminists and secular (non-religious) feminists, and that disconnect causes a lot of problems. Many religiously-minded feminists become offended at what they see as frankly ignorant critiques of their religion by secular feminists. Most recently, many debates have raged around Muslim women who constantly feel that they have to defend their ideals and religious beliefs to western feminists, especially with certain issues like choosing to wear a hijab.

When people face a traumatic event or experience in life they often seek solace in something they believe in, something that will offer potential solutions and fill the emotional and spiritual vacuum when everything else has failed.

The vastly daunting task to expand women's participation in society will be to dismantle centuries-old discrimination. The Islamic establishment to remove cultural obstacles sanctified by religious rulings.

The menace of "Forced and Child Marriage," females biggest conundrum

The infamous "Arabic Kalyanan" (Arab Wedding), a social malady prevalent in most parts of "Southern' Indian" province of "Kerela," this is an evil (inhuman) practice that has stirred up raging debate, which has devastated the lives of many young girls.

Poverty stricken parents particularly from backward Muslim community in Kerela, which could otherwise not meet the hefty dowry demand by local youths, are often used to be trapped by "visiting grooms" with the support of local marriage brokers and in many cases, by community elders.

Initially this supposedly rich "visiting grooms" entice and lure the brides with costly gifts like gorgeous apparels and gold ornaments and cash to lure their daughters into marriage.

Once marriage is solemnize after wedding the brides are taken on honeymoon trip for few days and even weeks, after which the groom would leave for their home abandoning the teenage bride to life of misery and tears.

To understand more about "forced and child marriage."

Child marriage is related to child **betrothal** and forced early marriage because of the pregnancy of the girl. In many cases, only one marriage-partner is a child, usually the female, due to importance placed upon female **virginity**. Child marriages are also driven by **poverty, bride price, dowry,** cultural traditions, laws that allow child marriages, **religious** and **social pressures,** regional customs, fear of remaining unmarried, illiteracy, and perceived inability of women to work for money.

Historically, child marriage was common around the world. The practice began to be questioned in the 20th century, with the age of individuals' first marriage increasing in many countries and most countries increasing the minimum marriage age. In ancient and medieval societies, it was common for girls to be betrothed at or even before puberty In Greece, early marriage and motherhood for girls was encouraged.

Forced and child marriages entrap women and young girls in relationships that deprive them of their basic human rights. Forced marriage constitutes a human rights violation in and of itself.

Forced marriages differ from arranged marriages. In forced marriages, one or both of the partners cannot give free or valid consent to the marriage. Forced marriages involve varying degrees of force, coercion or deception, ranging from emotional pressure by family or community members to abduction and imprisonment. Emotional pressure from a victim's family includes repeatedly telling the victim that the family's social standing and reputation are at stake, as well as isolating the victim or refusing to speak to her. In more severe cases, the victim can be subject to physical or sexual abuse, including rape.

Forced and child marriages have severe psychological, emotional, medical, financial, and legal consequences. Victims tend to be isolated from their peers and friends. They rarely have access to social services that could assist them. Early marriages often interrupt a victim's education. This deprives them of their right to education, as well as limits any possibility of economic independence from their spouse, making it more difficult to escape from an unwanted marriage. The unofficial nature of many of these marriages means that they often go unregistered, leaving a woman with no legal protections in cases of separation. Forced and child marriages are also more likely to become violent because the relationship is based on the power of one spouse over the other.

One in every five girls in the developing world is married by the age of 18. One in nine marries before they reach the age of 15. In countries like Niger, Chad, Mali, Bangladesh, Guinea and the Central African Republic (CAR), the rate of early and forced marriage is 60 per cent and over. Child brides are particularly prevalent in South Asia (46 per cent) and in sub-Saharan Africa (38 per cent).

Countries with the highest rates of early and forced marriage in Europe include Georgia (17 per cent), Turkey (14 per cent) and Ukraine (10 per cent). At least 10 per cent of adolescents marry before the age of 18 in Britain and France.

Marriage is a formalised, binding partnership between consenting adults. Child marriage involves either one or both spouses being children and may take place under civil, religious or customary laws with or without formal registration. A child is usually someone under 18.

Women and girls often occupy a lower status in societies as a result of social and cultural traditions, attitudes, beliefs that deny them their rights and stifle their ability to play an equal role in their homes and communities, in families on a low income, girls may be viewed as an economic burden. The perception of girls' potential to earn an income as comparatively poor pushes girls out of their homes and into marriage in many countries the importance of preserving family 'honour' and girls' virginity is such that parents push their daughters into marriage well before they are ready. There is a belief that marriage safeguards against 'immoral' or 'inappropriate behaviour.

In countries such as Afghanistan Despite some progress in women's rights such as guaranteeing equal rights for both men and women in the new constitution, the day-to-day life of women has changed little. Forced marriages and child marriages still continue and lead some women to escape their fate by choosing self-immolation.

Forced prostitution: Human trafficking, especially of girls and women, often leads to forced prostitution and sexual slavery. Forced prostitution is a crime against the person because of the violation of the victim's rights of movement through coercion and because of their commercial exploitation. Besides the elements of shame, ostracism, and physical injury, survivors of sexual assault are often burdened with a dependent child as a result of the rape.

Trafficking is the practice that delivers women and children into sexual exploitation. The number of women trafficked for this purpose is unknown, although conservative estimates put the number in the millions. Women do not voluntarily put themselves in situations where they are exploited, beaten, raped and enslaved. Women do not traffic themselves. Criminals who recruit, buy and sell women and girls are the crucial intermediaries for delivering women into prostitution. Traffickers supply the necessary elements for travel, such as money, documents, and connections in other countries. Traffickers are paid a sum of money for each woman and girl they deliver to a brothel or pimp. They use force, coercion, seduction, deception, and any other techniques that are effective in controlling the women and girls they are trading.

Prostitution is not the world's oldest profession, as is commonly said, although it is probably one of the world's oldest forms of men's violence against women and girls. It seems old because men's sexual exploitation of women and children is ancient and defended as a part of men's natures that they have to have sex, even if it is purchased, forced or with a child. Prostitution is not natural or inevitable; it is abuse and exploitation of women and girls that results from structural inequality between women and men on a world scale. Prostitution Commodifies women and girls and markets their bodies for whatever acts men have sexualized and want to buy. Rarely are adult men treated this way.

Truly the darkest and most powerful of the crimson arts is the seduction of women through the identifying and exploiting of their weaknesses and insecurities. To bed a woman is a wonderful pleasure, but to get inside her head and manipulate her to willingly offer the key to her heart — well, that is sublime gratification. Only experts in the mechanics of the human psyche can pull off Exploitation Game with any credibility.

Economic necessity, lack of employment option, drug addiction or coercion by family, pimps or trafficker, are all factors that can force women into sexual slavery. Paradoxically, it's the countries with the most straitlaced and sexually conservative societies, such as India, Pakistan or Iran, that have disproportionately large numbers of forced prostitutes. Since having sex with girlfriend may not be a viable option for most men in these cultures, prostitutes have become an acceptable solution.

Many in forced prostitution may also be subject to debt bondage, and charged excessive amount for travel, visas, food, accommodation, room hire and leaving expenses. Some women may be forced to service 800 men sexually just to clear their initial debt.

Once a girl or women enters prostitution it can be hard to leave it, it's not uncommon for pimps to use variety of methods to force women to continue serving as prostitutes. Often, they lure girls with alcohol or drugs, build up their dependency and use this addiction as means to control. They may also threatens girls with the shame they might bring on their families if they leave or the punishment they might suffer if they go to the police.

The Internet has become a site for the global sexual exploitation of women and children. In the past five years, sex industries have been the leaders in opening up the Internet for business. The Internet is almost without regulation because its international reach has made local and national laws and standards either obsolete or unenforceable. In addition, governments, such as the United States, decided on a "hands-off" policy to allow the sex industry almost unfettered operation on the Internet. With new types of technology, pornographers have introduced new ways to exploit and abuse women. With the techniques of videoconferencing, live sex shows are broadcast in which men dictate the performances of the women.

Chapter 6

There is a country in the Middle East where 10 percent of the population is denied equal rights because of their Race, where black men are not allowed to hold many government positions, where black women are put on trial for witchcraft and where the custody of children is granted to the parent with the most "racially superior" bloodline.

This Apartheid State is so enormously powerful that it controls American foreign policy in the Middle East even as its princes and princesses bring their slaves to the United Kingdom and the United States. **That country is Saudi Arabia.** Saudi Arabia abolished slavery in 1962 under pressure from President Kennedy, who accomplished what the Ottoman Empire and the League of Nations had not been able to, but that hasn't stopped its citizens from selling castrated slaves on social media site "Facebook" or its princes from beating their black slaves to death in posh London hotels.

But Saudi Arabia's oil wealth eventually made slavery economically unnecessary. Early on, African slaves worked for foreign oil companies which paid their masters, but they were a poor fit for the oil economy. The Kingdom no longer needed agricultural slaves and pearl drivers; it needed trained technicians from the West and international travel made it cheaper to import Asian workers for household labour and construction than to maintain its old trade in slaves. The Saudis replaced the 450,000 slaves of the 1950s with 8.4 million guest workers.

It's a shame to humanity that even in this day and age of 21ˢᵗ century in times of digital age, the age old ancient era barbaric and heinous criminal method of punishing alleged culprits like "Stoning people to Death' vitriolic acid attack and Female Genital Mutilation" is prevalent in many countries and region.

History: Stoning is arguably the world's oldest form of execution. It is as old as written literature. Although it has never been a legal form of execution in the United States, but Stoning still happens today elsewhere. Stoning is an ancient practice that dates back to Ancient Greece. It did not originate from Islam. In fact, it did not originate from any religion. It appears as though it was created in Ancient Greek mythology. The point is not necessarily to identify how or where stoning originated but to give it context. It belongs to no religion, but how one interprets their religion, and applies those interpretations.

There are 15 countries in which stoning is either practiced or authorized by law, even if it has never been practiced. In Iran, Mauritania, Nigeria (in one-third of the country's states), Pakistan, Qatar, Saudi Arabia, Somalia, Sudan, the United Arab Emirates, and Yemen, stoning is a legal punishment. However, out of these countries, only in Iran, Pakistan and Somalia have stoning actually occurred, and all instances in Pakistan have occurred outside the legal system. By comparison, three of the remaining five countries (Afghanistan, Iraq, and Mali) do not condone stoning in national legislation, but sentences and executions have been carried out by non-state actors. In the Aceh region of Indonesia and Malaysia, stoning is sanctioned regionally but banned nationally.

Stoning is used as a punishment for adultery, or Zina. It is a method used to control the sexuality and bodies of both men and women, but women are more often the victims. The issue of stoning takes place within the much broader conversation about gender discrimination, women's basic freedoms and culturally-justified violence against women. Simply put, women are more likely to be found guilty of adultery than men – because the hegemonic interpretations of Islamic law, personal status laws, poverty, and illiteracy among women all increase the likelihood of their conviction, either in a court of law or by the community.

The prisoner is buried either up to his waist (if male) or up to her shoulders (if female) and then pelted with stones by a crowd of volunteers until obviously battered to death. Under the terms of most fundamentalist courts, the stones must be small enough that death cannot reasonably be expected to result from only one or two blows, but large enough to cause physical harm. The average execution by stoning is extremely painful, lasting at least 10 to 20 minutes.

Women's rights activists have launched an international campaign for a ban on stoning, which is mostly inflicted on women accused of adultery. Stoning is a cruel and hideous punishment. It is a form of torturing someone to death. It is one of the most brutal forms of violence perpetrated against women in order to control and punish their sexuality and basic freedoms.

Stoning is not legal in most Muslim countries and there is no mention of it in the "Quran" (Islam' Holy book). But supporters argue that it is legitimised by the Hadith – the acts and sayings of the Prophet Mohamed. Stoning is set out as a specific punishment for adultery under several interpretations of Sharia or Islamic law. In some instances, even a woman saying she has been raped can be considered an admission to the crime of Zina (sex outside marriage).

True, Islam or its founder "Prophet Mohammed" cannot be blame for this barbaric "Law" of stoning any humans to death, as it is an age old law which existed and was allegedly practice long before Prophet Mohammed was born, and this law of stoning human to death is not his thought at all.

But, Prophet Mohammed cannot be absolve as well because he in his life time, he had ordered the punishment of few individuals found to have committed adultery, as per historians it has been reported that; when Two people guilty of "illegal intercourse" were brought before "Mohammed" who commanded that they both be stoned. Apparently their act was out of love.

Then Prophet had also said that if, a married man confesses that he has Adultery, Prophet Mohammed orders the man be planted and pelted with stones.

Also it has been reported, **"The Adulterer Must be Stoned."** This words were a part of Prophet Mohammed farewell address to his people on the occasion of his final pilgrimage to Mecca.

Some of such incidents of this "Brutal and Barbaric' Law" worth discussing about which has occurred in recent past, one such incident, A Huge crowd helplessly and brazenly watched barbaric and brutal crime being committed outside a Lahore courthouse, the family of a pregnant Pakistani woman beat her to death because she married the man she loved instead of her cousin. The 25-year-old (Farzana Praveen) woman's father, brother and spurned fiancé were among about a dozen male relatives who used bricks and clubs in the so-called honour killing of Farzana Parveen for disobeying her family's wishes. She suffered massive head injuries and was pronounced dead at a hospital. Farzana Parveen was attacked as she and her husband, Mohammad Iqbal, arrived at the gates of the Lahore High Court. They went there to dispute charges brought by her father that Iqbal had kidnapped Parveen, who had been engaged to her cousin for several years.

This casual bargain between blood relations over a dead body of a female relative is what Farzana Parveen's family is counting on as well. On May 27-2014, when 25-year-old **Farzana Parveen** was brutally killed with bricks outside the Lahore High Court, condemnations came pouring in through international and domestic press. This uproar against the killing was loud enough that the Pakistani prime minister eventually "took notice."

This incident is even more horrendous, for a rather bizarre reason a woman in Pakistan "Miss Arifa Bibi" a young mother of two was stoned to death by her relatives on the order of a tribal court in Pakistan. Her crime: possession of a **"Mobile Phone."** Arifa Bibi's uncle, cousins and others hurled stones and bricks at her until she died, according to media reports. She was buried in a desert far from her village. It's unlikely anyone was arrested. Her case is not unique.

The furore over the bad publicity for Pakistan and the fact that they were being painted as a society tolerant of barbaric acts such as killings, has also resulted in a few clerics who call themselves moderate declaring "fatwas", or Islamic edicts, against killing women in the name of honour.

In Iraq a 17 year old girl Du'a Khalil Aswad was brutally stoned to death, "an abhorrent murder," her fault was that she felt in love with a teenage boy who was from different religion, to her dismay, Miss Aswad while she was being stoned to death the local city Iraqi security force witnessed the incident of Du'a being stoned to death yet did nothing to stop it, Miss Aswad, a member of minority Kurdish group called Yezidi, was condemned to death as "Honour killing" by other men in her family and other Hardline religious leaders because of her intimate relationship with a boy who was from Sunni Muslim community, Du'a Khalil Aswad was drag outside her house by 8 or 9 men and was stoned for nearly half an hour till she died.

Such incident of stoning young girls and women are becoming more common, extreme barbaric sharia laws are practiced in the jihadist (holy warrior) terrorist group ISIS controlled areas in Iraq and Syria, many incident of stoning girls to death are videotaped and released on social media site like Youtube.

Over the past 100 years or more, many feminist movement have strived hard to win battle of wits against their opposite sex gender. Women have indeed made significant progress, girls and women are doing remarkably well professionally, they have high income jobs, women are skilled professionals and owns businesses, whether in fashion world or corporate world, even in agriculture or Aerospace women have found space for themselves and many a females have become principle breadwinners for their family, despite all that women have proved they are No less courageous and are equally competitive in almost every field and arena as good as men or maybe given a chance to prove they could prove to be more productive than men. But, yet, with heavy heart I have to say, that even in this day and age around the world most people are living with generations old primitive mind set, particularly in highly densely populated countries like India and Pakistan you will find extremely backward thinking outrageously superstitious and savagely conservative people.

In countries such as India and Pakistan most people belonging to either affluent class or underclass social background, talk about economically backward or wealthy families, they are both equal offenders and on same page when it comes to thinking with regards to girl child, most of the people particularly in India and Pakistan subtly, covertly or overtly considers birth of a girl child in their families as jinx and inauspicious, their insular beliefs considers it is a curse to have girl child born into their family, many parents considers girl child to be burden on them as they believe daughters are liability for their parents, because girls are no good and can't become breadwinners for their family, therefore you will read and listen lots of real life stories of brazen and brutal parents of beleaguered infant girl child in countries like India, Pakistan or even Afghanistan ruthlessly getting Rid of their infant daughter by either killing infant girl child or throw her in Trash-bin or leaves her on railway platform as soon as she's born, the killings are executed in most dreadful manner, shameless and callous parents don't hesitate one bit in killing their daughter by stoning her to death using grinding stone or smash her to wall, gosh, it is really horrendous but to our dismay, it is true, that, parents kills or get rid of their daughters in bizarrely inhuman and barbaric of way, it is a heart rending fact.

There is nothing in any religious book which sanctions honour killing but even then Hundreds, if not thousands, of women are murdered by their families each year in the name of family "honour." It's difficult to get precise numbers on the phenomenon of honour killing, the murders frequently go unreported, the perpetrators unpunished, and the concept of family honour justifies the act in the eyes of some societies. Honour Killing concept came to light in India just because the media highlighted the issue with responsibility. But the concept is not new its existence is as old as society. The reason behind the honour killing is still same i.e. women are considered as a vessel of the family reputation.

"Honour" works to restrict women's autonomy, particularly sexual autonomy within male-dominated societies which place a high value on women's chastity. Within "honour" crimes, families may collaborate to commit violence against a relative who is thought to have violated the restrictions around female behaviour. Such violations might include dress or make-up which is not approved by the family, resisting an arranged marriage, seeking divorce, reporting domestic violence and some so-called offences may appear trivial.

Honour killings most often involve young women attempting to break from the pre-modern cultural traditions of their immigrant families — families plunged into the maelstrom of increasingly post-modern secular society. (The occasional male victims tend to be accused of adultery and homosexuality as well as rape, exhibitionism and paedophilia.) In most cases, perpetrators of honour killings appear motivated by deeply held moral convictions and seek to restrict the influence of Western values, especially involving dress, socialisation and sexuality.

The stoning of women is one of the most savage, and revealing aspect of the Mullah's in Iran. This vicious punishment of women is without precedent in Iran recent history. Since the inception of the Mullah's rule, hundreds of women of various ages have been continue to be stoned to death throughout Iran. The responsibility for any inhuman punishment regardless of where it takes place, lies with the judiciary and the state.

This incident puts humanity to the ultimate shame, how inhuman some among we humans can be, as reported in newspaper and in media, On August 10, 1994, in the city of Arak, a woman was sentenced to death by stoning. According to the ruling of the religious judge, her husband and two children were forced to attend the execution. The woman urged her husband to take the children away, but to no avail. A truck full of stones was brought in to be used during the stoning. In the middle of the stoning, although her eyes had been gouged out, the victim was able to escape from the ditch and started running away, but the regime's guards recaptured her and shot her to death.

Now explicitly speaking, How ridiculous it is, what is so honourable or dishonourable about, if someone wants to love somebody who he/she thinks is compatible, why can't each citizen enjoy basic civil rights and have freedom of choice and expression? Is it fair or for the parents to interfere in their children's personal life particularly their love-life, why not each adult grown up children whether its son or daughter have fundamental right to choose life-partner or spouse of their own choice, should the parents especially in case of their daughter threaten their daughter of dire consequences if she wish to marry to a boy of her own choice, in extreme cases or in more conservative societies parents strongly objects to their daughter/daughters choice of marrying or intimate relationship with a boy whom they love consider compatible because parents takes into consideration boy's caste and religion he belongs to as well his social and economic status and if that doesn't match then parents considers relation as mismatch and treats their daughters choice and allege lover as pariah.

Let's understand it,

"For example: A) if a girl from devout Muslim family falls in love with a Non-Muslim boy and wants to marry him. B) A daughter of a wealthy rich parents falls in love with a boy who is a truck driver or a waiter in a restaurant, in either of these two scenario will the parents consider that their beloved daughter is bring disrespect and dishonouring their family's pride and lowering dignity hence the parents will by force or by persuasion and muscle power try to dissuade their daughter from marrying a boy of her choice or else they will go to any extend take extreme step to stop her in her bid to take relationship with her intimate lover man to next level which is marrying him, so to halt her from moving forward parents will take law into their own hands and punish their daughter by brutally stoning her to death or by any mean eliminating their daughter without any remorse if she doesn't fall in line with her parents wish." Vicious world, selfish people have double standards, the more you answer such questions the more questions keeps arising.

Well, Parents would be better advised of playing an advisory role, rather than taking law into their own hands, by taking extreme steps of harming their children particularly in case of dealing their daughter's personal life issues. Most parents likes taking total control and command of their children's life and profoundly keeps interfering in every matter and outrageously prevents their children from taking decisions concerning their personal life on their own, which at times results in discord between children and parents, often in such pressurized situations the children becomes rebels and adopts violent and aggressive approach or they suffer extreme mental pain and depression and thoroughly lose confidence in themselves and their mental balance.

Jilted lover, one sided love affair, voracious husband who is unhappy because his wife has not met his dowry demand or if husband suspects his wife of Adultery, or drug addict/alcoholic or religious fundamentalist stubborn insular faming brother and father: these are those uncanny reasons and it becomes catalyst for men to commit one of the most inhuman and wickedest of crime a human can ever think of or commit, that is; **Acid Attack a Woman with intention to Disfigure her beautiful Looks**: Acid attack a vitriol attack or Vitriolage is a form of violent attack. This crime oft committed by a disgruntled person/persons (specially, mostly are found to be man who either with help of his associates or his family members) to teach woman a lesson of her life to ruin her life once end for all, this crime otherwise committed all over the world but it is particularly common in countries like Pakistan, Afghanistan, Bangladesh and India, defined as the act of throwing **acid** or a similarly **corrosive substance** onto the body of another "with the intention to **disfigure, maim, torture**, or kill. It's a shocking crime, no matter where it's committed. Acid thrown in someone's face, leaving the victim burned, maimed and disfigured. Sadly, it happens more often than you think around the globe, and almost always, the victims are women. Perpetrators of these attacks throw acid at their victims, usually at their faces, burning them, and damaging skin tissues, often exposing and sometimes dissolving the bones. The long term consequences of these attacks may include blindness, as well as permanent scarring of the face and body, along with far-reaching social, psychological, and economic difficulties. The most common types of acid used in these attacks are sulphuric and nitric acid. Hydrochloric acid is sometimes used, but is much less damaging.

The reasoning behind heinous attacks is even more disturbing. Frequently, they occur because a woman wants a divorce from an abusive husband and he seeks to bring shame upon her for taking action against him. Steps are being taken to improve laws and prosecution for these crimes yet acid attack continues to be on rise. To elaborate further; Most acid-attacks are punishing measures towards women who have refused to accede to commands from men or have stood against abuses from them. The effects of these acid attacks upon their lives have been destructive: apart from the physical trauma undergone (some are scarred and maimed for life, despite numerous surgical interventions), they also have to face psychological trauma as well as social isolation and ostracism from their community. A law against acid crimes will hardly act as a deterrent when perpetrators know that if they have enough resources and leverage than they can shrug off any charge held against them, no matter the atrocity.

From the victims' point of view, there is a high risk of denial of justice, and the numerous obstacles they can face in their pursuit of justice may act as a strong disincentive preventing them from reporting the attacks. Indeed, the status of women in Pakistan, subject on the one hand to pressures not to disgrace their families by filing a case, and on the other hand, to disdain from the police officers themselves, will add to the obstacles faced by any average Pakistani seeking justice within a corrupted policing system and administration. Acid attacks are reported in many parts of the world. Since 1990s, Bangladesh has been reporting the highest number of attacks and highest incidence rates for women.

In addition to medical and psychological effects, many social implications exist for acid attack survivors, especially women. For example, such attacks usually leave victims handicapped in some way, rendering them dependent on either their spouse or family for everyday activities, such as eating and running errands. These dependencies are increased by the fact that many acid survivors are not able to find suitable work, due to impaired vision and physical handicap. This negatively impacts their economic viability, causing hardships on the families/spouses that care for them. As a result, divorce rates are high, with abandonment by husbands found in 25% acid assault cases in Uganda (compared to only 3% of wives abandoning their disfigured husbands. In some countries such as Saudi Arabia, Bahrain and Kuwait, acid attack victims are psychologically persecuted after the acid attack. The media overwhelmingly avoids reporting acid attack related violence; if covered, the description of the attack is minimized, blames the victims, omits women's voices, and treats sympathetically men who commit these crimes.

It has been reported on **Media News channel "CNN": "**It's the latest cruel tactic in the Pakistani Taliban's battle to stop girls and women from getting an education: acid thrown in their faces to scare them for life and deter others from following in their footsteps. The Pakistani Taliban have taken responsibility for the attacks and threatening pamphlets distributed around the city of Parachinar. They also warn local girls against going to school, "We will never allow the girls of this area to go and get a Western education," said Qari Muhavia, the local Pakistani Taliban leader, when contacted by CNN (media News Channel) by telephone. "If and when we find any girl from Parachinar going to university for an education we will target her (in) the same way, so that she might not be able to unveil her face before others," Muhavia said.

Shahab Uddin, a local government official from Kurram Agency in Pakistan's northern tribal belt, said the acid attack was the latest method used to terrorize young girls and deter them from going to school. Two girls, Zahida and Nabila, and one more boy had suffered burns, Uddin said, while Mohammad Ali, a fourth boy, was the student who was shot. "After throwing acid on the students the assailants opened fire on the van," Uddin said."-----CNN.-------

"Women is a Nature's Best Creation, hence, Discriminating Women is equal to Discriminating' Mother Nature."

Heart rending isn't it, how can we humans or least some among us be so cruel and callous? Ever wondered, just a small stone hits me/us it pains so damn much at times we have to go to doctor's clinic for bandages, now, just imagine a person being stoned to death or hazardous flammable Acid thrown on face, because more often than not, the victims of these most barbaric crimes are young girls and women. We can only imagine the pain and agony of those people who have to bear such ferocious brutality of being stoned to death or suffering acid attacks.

But these crimes are not the only types of crimes perpetrated, there are many other types of crimes and harassments as well.

As we discussed and talked about family's honour and dishonour, another related questions comes in mind again a very controversial topic to debate here I'm talking about **Incest;** like it is always difficult to define terrorism similarly it is as difficult to define <u>Incest</u> because incest for some in the society is considered to be a taboo, a stigma, but there are many who find nothing wrong in some form of incest, some religions accept that Sex between certain close relatives is not wrong and should not be stigmatized. In simple term Incest means Sex performed between either family members or very close blood relatives. Now, various Religions have separate Rules for Incest they justifies certain form of Incest while contemporary legal law system in most countries differ dramatically with regards to Rules set by various religions, hence the legal law system doesn't approve of many forms of Incest and has declared it criminal act thereby punishable.

But Incest is a practice as old as recorded human history, in ancient era, incest was common in many civilization of the world.

Incest is **sexual activity** between family members or close **relatives.** This typically includes sexual activity between people in a **consanguineous** relationship (blood relations), and sometimes those related by **affinity**, such as members of the same **household step relatives**, those related by **adoption** or **marriage**, or members of the same **clan** or **lineage**. The **incest taboo** is and has been one of the most widespread of all cultural **taboos**, both in present and in many past societies. Most modern societies have **laws regarding incest** or social restrictions on closely consanguineous marriages.

Several of the Egyptian **Pharaohs** married their siblings and had several children with them. (For example, **Tutankhamun** married his half-sister **Ankhesenamun**. Tutankhamun himself was the child of an incestuous union between **Akhenaten** and an unidentified sister-wife). It is now generally accepted that sibling marriages were widespread among all classes in Egypt during the Graeco-Roman period. Numerous **papyri** and the Roman census declarations attest to many husbands and wives being brother and sister, of the same father and mother. The most famous of these relationships were in the royal family, the Ptolemies; Cleopatra VII was married to her younger brother, Ptolemy XIII. Her mother and father, **Cleopatra V** and Ptolemy XII, had also been brother and sister. According to Genesis 20:12 of the Hebrew Bible. The Patriarch Abraham and his wife Sarah were half-siblings, both being children of Terah, but with different mothers.

We all seem to know that incest is wrong, either through cultural conditioning or what appear to be innate evolutionary cues, yet some humans can't seem to resist the urge to bed their relatives. In fact, since the DNA of every living human is **99.9 percent the same**, it may be **much more common** than we think. Still, that doesn't mean incest is a good thing. As we will see, breeding with a close relative can result in some dire consequences.

Even if you believe that two consenting adults should be able to have sex with whomever they please, there's no escaping the fact that reproducing with a close relative has some serious drawbacks. When we mate with someone with a completely different gene pool, our chance of passing on **Recessive genes** is only 50 percent. Many times, those genes remain dormant, but when people who share a large number of genes breed, the chance of passing on conditions known as autosomal recessive disorders—conditions that are inherited through recessive genes, including cystic fibrosis, sickle cell anaemia, and albinism—increases significantly. Other side effects of inbreeding include the increased risk of infertility, birth defects like cleft palates, heart conditions, facial asymmetry, low birth weight, slow growth rate, and neonatal mortality. One study found that 40 percent of children whose parents were first-degree relatives were born with autosomal recessive disorders, congenital physical malformations, or severe intellectual deficits.

Most people find incest unacceptable, and there are compelling reasons for such a position: (1) culturally and traditionally, incest is largely considered a taboo, and (2) inbreeding — those with close genetic relationships producing offspring — greatly increases the chance of the child/children developing congenital disorders. Incest has, however, occurred quite often in history, the royalty of ancient Egypt using it as a means of perpetuating their royal lineage. Today though, incest is considered a crime in most territories with only a few countries like the Netherlands, Spain, and France being exceptions. In fact, even in these countries where consensual incest is legal, the public is still largely outraged by such relationships despite the fact that the state tolerates them.

Most religions have flawed set of rules, the purpose of debate should not be to debase or disparage any particular religion or religions, as well as not to criticise the founder of any particular religious faith, but there should be honest assessment and frank discussion to establish the truth, fact should prevail, so as to, safeguard the interest of coming generations thereby to save them from the menace of such social ills like Incest.

With regards to religions, Islam double standard exposed and its religious theology subject to more thorough scrutiny because the Islamists particularly the Sunni-Muslim faction of Islam consider themselves to be supremely purest and most close to divine. The Islamist people mince no words in voicing disparaging comments and views to defame every other religion and also do not spare the agnostic/atheist belief, they very emphatically call people from every other religious communities and non-believers **Kafir** (Infidels) and considers all non-believers of Islam as followers of evil, the Islamist community people are of the opinion that harming the Infidels is not a sin but by doing so they are serving the purpose of Allah (Islam god) and their prophet.

Article titled; **"Islam- The Crimes of Prophet Mohammed"** stated: **"Muslims are sanctified by the blood of murdered kafirs (Infidels).**

What is important to understand is that none of these depraved, criminal acts are crimes to Muslims. They are all holy, divine acts to be emulated by all Muslim men. They are all Sunna [The traditional portion of Muslim law based on Muhammad's words or acts, accepted (together with the Koran) as authoritative by Muslims].

- Molested his wife – six-year-old Baby Aisha. One of Baby Aisha's wifely duties was to clean semen stains from the prophet's clothes. The prophet Mohammed would take a bath with Baby Aisha and thigh with Baby Aisha taking his penis and rubbing it up and down her thighs. Being a man of mercy he did not penetrate Baby Aisha until she was nine.
- Raped Baby Aisha when she was nine (texts can have been altered to change the age. Koranic texts claim he married her when she was six and he may have consummated the marriage then as well. Reason for this being that other indications in the Hadith shows that Mohammed was a Paedophile). Advocated sex with baby girls.

- Captured women and raped them. Kept women as sex slaves. Muhammad had sex with 61 women: many he raped. There is no consensual sex between a child girl and a man. There is no consensual sex between a master and his sex slave. There is no consensual sex between a woman conquered in war and her husband conqueror. All such sexual acts are rape. RAPE IS RAPE.
- Had eleven wives at one time. Sexually abused his wives. Raped his wives. Forced sex during their menstruation including Baby Aisha. Mentally abused his wives. Can you imagine taking a child (or any aged woman) and molesting with your hand/fist her menstruating vagina?

References: [h/t Craig]
–

Muhammad's marriage to 6yr old Aisha-(Sahih Al-Bukhari, Volume 5, Book 58, Number 234 and 236).

– Aisha cleans Muhammad's semen stains-(Sahih Al-Bukhari, Volume 1, Book 4, Number 229-233),

– Muhammad fondling Aisha during her 'Menses'- (Sahih al-Bukhari, Volume 1, Book 6, Number 298-300, Sunan Abu Dawud, Book 1, Number 0270)

– Muhammad liked to have intercourse with Aisha and his other wives when they were menstruating (Sahih Muslim, Book 003, Number 0577-0579),......."
Islam – The Crimes of Prophet Mohammed.".....

In one of the survey it was found; Islam under the guise of Sharia law and the Quran endorses rape of women, and incest of infants and children. The effect of this is a massive number of sexual assault cases on women and children.

Over 23% of Muslim children in a University study claimed to have been raped (1/4 of the entire population). Over 46% of Muslim male students in Riyadh are homosexuals, and over 25% of Muslim male student in Jeddah are homosexuals. Homosexual relations are common due to restriction of association   between   genders. The actual percentage of sexual assault on children and women, beyond this University study, is believed to be over 80%.

In the study, it was mentioned that more than 16% of the rapists were relatives, specifically 5% were siblings, 2% were teachers, and 1% were parents. In another study, which was conducted by Dr. In'am (al-Rabu'i), who is the president of children's studies at the Armed Forces Hospital in Jeddah, she mentioned, or warned, that in the coming years we will suffer as a society from extremely widespread cases of homosexuality. The reason for this is the increase in the cases of sexual assault of children (brought) to the hospital, as well as the societal violence inflicted on children. She also mentioned that the hospital had on average three sexual assault cases per week.

Here I would like to add, that, Incest is a global Phenomena and it persists across the geographic and demographic almost every religion touches base with it. In Hindu Mythology wherein the ancient epic "Mahabharata" princess **Draupadi** was under rather bizarre and exceptional circumstances was married to Five brothers "Pandava's," worse still to her dismay in one of the social gatherings in the palace at Hastinapur (in' North-India) her husbands gambled and put her at stake and lost her in Dice hall assembly and as result of which Draupadi was brazenly and callously Disrobed by the cousin of her husbands the "Kauravas" in large conclave in Hastinapur in front of Hundreds of people.

Also sexual discrimination in Christianity cannot be overlooked, Pope's of many generations have publicly accepted and tendered public apologies for committed heinous crimes of sexual abuse and exploitation of infancy children as well of beleaguered women also many investigating reports and victims revelation have stated of consensual sex between Nuns and Priest in various Christians religious institutions.

When others harm us, we complain a lot, but, when we are hurt and harmed by our own people, what do we do? Keep quite and maintain stoic silence, tolerate all the pain, this is what many people do. No wonder, why many surveys and studies conducted by several human rights activists and organizations have found that **Domestic Violence** is worse than conventional Military warfare. We people at times are not safe among our own folks, to say the least. Another perspective, ill-timed and reckless decisions besides bad choices lack of knowledge and understanding of pressing ground realities people are self-destructive they destroy their own life, or their life is destroyed by their own family members or close relatives and friends. It is so, that, our fierce enemy at times can't or won't harm us as much we harm our own-self, it is human nature that we have habit of never admitting our own mistakes, we never admit or agree doing wrong instead we always blame others for our own wrongdoings.

Another form of atrocities against women is "Sexualize terror, rape as weapon of war: "Rape is a particular form of violence against women which, while not always fatal, often leaves women physically and emotionally scarred for rest of her life. Rape is used as a strategy of war: "The world woke up to this phenomenon in 1993, after discovering that Serbian forces had set up a network of 'rape camps' in which women and girls, some as young as 12, were enslaved. Since then, we've seen similar patterns of systematic rape in many countries, and it has become clear that mass rape is not just a by-product of war but also sometimes a deliberate weapon.

The 1990s war in the former Yugoslavia was marked by intense sexualized violence that ruined the lives of old women and young girls alike, Bosnian Serbs were responsible for the majority of sexualized attacks, aimed mostly at Muslim women. It is estimated that as many as 60,000 women were raped. There are testimonies from women who had soldiers tell them, while raping them, that they wanted to get them pregnant or force them to have children who would look ethnically different from their mother, or that they were raping them to punish them for being Muslim (or Croatian). There were also women who became pregnant and were **forced to carry their babies** to term.

Many women were raped in front of their children and husbands, who were forced to watch at gunpoint; there are also a fair number of accounts of elderly women who were raped (in those cases, it was clearly not about impregnating them but about demeaning them and their families). Thousands of males were forced to engage in sexual acts with other males, including, according to some accounts, their own father or son.

In Sudan, the government has turned all of Darfur into a rape camp, typically, the women are scarred or branded, or occasionally have their ears cut off. In some areas of eastern Congo three-quarters of women have been raped, sometimes with pointed sticks that leave the victims incontinent from internal injuries.

Article title **"Sexual Terror: Untold Stories of Beslan Jihad"** ------ "On September 1, 2004, Islamist terrorist sent by the Chechen terrorist warlord Shamil Basayev, the terrorists stormed a school in Beslan, Russia, and perpetrated one of the most heinous terror attacks in history. Though many people may have heard of this attack, it is very likely that most do not know what really happened there. The reality is so dark that few dare speak of what went on.
There are predators in wait lurking everywhere searching for unsuspecting victims. If a person has a proclivity or a secret desire, that inclination can easily come out if an opportunity arises. And that is what happened at Beslan. The terrorists immediately killed the men because they wanted no resistance for their plans. Then, when they saw the helpless girls in front of them, the temptation became too much. Their perverse dreams came true.

Beslan was clearly a sexual homicide/sexual suicide. That is, the offenders wanted more than simple terrorism. Some of the terrorists at Beslan were hired guns who did not plan on dying that day. They had not thought things through and did not realize that the Russians would not let them out alive. Then, once they were inside, and the realization dawned on them, plans changed.

Things had deteriorated when the media reported that there were only 354 victims. Wanting to have a dramatic impact, the terrorists exploded with anger. There were 1200 victims, and the Russians were trying to down play the incident. The terrorists said they would have to eliminate victims to fit with what the media had reported. Their demeanour worsened, and they got really mean.

It was then that they began raping the girls. They wanted sex as they killed, and this is sexual homicide. A sex killer gets excited when he thinks about forcing himself inside an unwilling victim, but the rape itself does not produce the ultimate excitement. It is the rape followed by the killing that is arousing. This is what happened at Beslan. One by one, females were targeted. The sex killers looked for the perfect victims, and after zeroing in, they grabbed and disrobed the little girls in the middle of the gym. There were muffled cries as the girls were humiliated in front of everyone. They were stripped, raped, and sodomized by several men Not content to simply rape, the terrorists used their guns and other objects to penetrate the screaming victims while the other hostages were forced to watch. And the terrorists laughed. They laughed as they violated the children and made them bleed. What few people know is that some of the girls died as a result of being raped with objects."--------------

"Muslim men who fear being seduced or tempted into immoral behaviour by the beauty of their female servants, or even of those servants "casting spells" on them, would be better to purchase women from an "enslaved maid" agency for sexual purposes. What is required of is to set up special offices which could be set up to provide concubines in the same way as domestic staff recruitment agencies currently provide housemaids. "For the youth to be protected from adultery."

Since 1996, more than six million people have been killed in the continuing war in the Democratic Republic of Congo (DCR or Congo). As London-based academic Carrie Giunta points out, the ongoing annihilation of humanity in the DCR exceeds by millions the number of deaths engineered over the same timeframe through war and conflict in Darfur, Iraq, Afghanistan, Bosnia and Rwanda. The vast majority killed in the Congo are civilians. Not since WW II have so many deaths occurred through the deliberate and consequential killing that follows the declaration of war. Rape and sexual torture have featured prominently in the Congo's killing fields. Occurring on a daily basis, militia strategically turn the bodies of females of all ages, some infants, others elderly, into battle grounds. They do this by penetrating and mutilating their victim's genitals to impart maximum physical and psychological damage. The damage to victims, and also to their families and communities, is not only horrific. It is immeasurable. It happens alongside kidnapping which, while targeting young men as military recruits, also targets girls and women for sex slavery. Often, women and girls are held captive for months or, in some instances, for several years.

Sex Slavery in the Quran and Hadiths

Abu Dawud – in his Hadith Collection (2150) "The Apostle of Allah 'Prophet Mohammed' sent a military expedition to Awtas on the occasion of the battle of Hunain. They met their enemy and fought with them. They defeated them and took them captives. Some of the Companions of the Apostle of Allah Prophet Mohammed were reluctant to have **intercourse with the female captives in the presence of their husbands** who were unbelievers (Non-Muslims). So Allah, the Exalted, sent down the Qur'anic verse: (Qur'an 4:24) 'And all married women (are forbidden) unto you save those (captives) whom your right hands possess.'" This is the background for verse 4:24 of the Qur'an. Not only does Allah grant permission for women to be captured and raped, but allows it to even be done in front of their husbands."........

Would you join a religion that permitted men to have sex with their slave-girls throughout their enslavement—if this religion codified this act in its holy book?

Many persons in the West (and elsewhere) who convert to Islam are women. Would women do this if they knew about ALL of this religion? Reasonable women should stop and think a second time before taking this serious step (but a reversible one, albeit punishable by death in many Islamic countries).

Islam goes more deeply than just the benign Five Pillars. It has many unpleasant truths lurking in its sacred texts. The goal of this article is to bring out yet another of these truths, so people can make *fully* informed decisions from *all* of the facts.

"Who created whom? Humans created God a figment of our imagination or god created human beings." Is God real or Myth, the issue of whether God is Real or just a fictional character in the human drama, well this issue is inconclusively being discussed and debated for who knows how many thousands of years. However it is true that of all the genders, male or female "Gay or Straight" the women gender is found to be the most religious and spiritual, the women's since generations are supposedly devout and dedicated worshippers and firm believers in concept of God again across geographic and demographics and in every religion whether Monotheism or Paganism, female gender solemnly religious yet the women are discriminated most in every religion, almost every religion so-called Holy-books preaching and teachings are nothing but unholiest and bias towards women particularly the Monotheist religions holy-books so outrageously exploits and discriminates women.

Biggest discrimination against women is when she bleeds for those few days of the month as in many cultures and societies **menstruation is considered a taboo,** In some societies it involves menstruation being perceived as unclean or embarrassing, extending even to the mention of menstruation both in public and in private (amongst the friends, in the household, and with men). In Hinduism as well as in Islam and Judaism once a girl reaches puberty they are barred from entering prayer room and stopped from performing prayers or any other rituals in fact in some traditional Hindu and Islamic families menstruating girls and women are barred from entering kitchen and not allowed to cook food or wash clothes till there menstrual cycle ends, because many traditional religions considers menstruation **ritually unclean.** Backward thinking insular religious people firmly believes that menstruating women whatever things she touches gets contaminated. Considering a woman unclean while she is <u>bleeding (menstruating)</u> is patriarchal hogwash simply a superstition without any rational basis all nonsense.

Not just religions are very harmful but detrimental to human progress. Religion breeds patriarchy, leading to misogyny and incredible violence it causes to women. My advice to women's will be that women must invest more time in themselves and strive to empower themselves rather wasting precious time and resources looking up in the sky waiting for divine intervention to bless them, women desperately needs to develop cognitive and technical skills so that they can gain economic independence and do not have to rely on others.

A new concept emerge in the so-called Arab Spring conflict **"Sex – Jihad"** when, one of the leading Islamic clerics in Saudi Arabia, Sheikh Muhammad al-'Arifi, issued a fatwa (religious ruling) authorizing Muslim women and girls from all over the world to travel to **Syria** to surrender their bodies to rebel fighters so as to relieve their pent-up sexual frustration while attempting to establish Sunni-Islam caliphate in Iraq and Syria. A fatwa that allowed teenage girls to provide sexual relief for rebels battling the Syrian President "Assad's" forces.

Jihad al-Nikah, (Jihad al-Nikah is an Arabic phrase meaning "sexual holy war,") permitting extramarital sexual relations with multiple partners, is considered by some hard-line Sunni Muslim Salafists as a legitimate form of holy war.

Muslim women prostituting themselves would be considered legitimate because they are making sacrifices "giving away their chastity and dignity" to help the Jihadis.

Why some women would obey such an order is less clear, but one expert suggests they may believe it's an act of devotion. "Muslim women prostituting themselves in this case is being considered a legitimate jihad because such women are making sacrifices—their chastity, their dignity—in order to help apparently sexually-frustrated Jihadis better focus on the war to empower Islam in Syria."

Gruesome revelation in "Reports" of Tunisian women **travelling to Syria to** "wage sex jihad" emerged in 2013 after interior minister Lofti Ben Jeddou told MPs that thousands of women had sexual relations with "20, 30, 100 militants" in war-torn Syria. "After **the sexual liaisons they have there in the name of 'jihad al-Nikah,'** they come home pregnant," he said.

Thousands of girls from countries such as "Egypt, Somalia and Tunisia" who've offered their bodies for the purpose of sexual – Jihad and travelled to countries like Syria to sleep with the Jihadist, most among those girls and women apart from unwanted pregnancy they have contracted serious sex related aliment and disease like "HIV' Aids."

The sexual Jihad Fatwa made its first appearance in Syria, when it allowed for armed members to have sexual intercourse with women for a determined period of time as per a momentary contract that loses effect after a few hours.

This will allow other men to sign a similar contract and women to sleep with more than one man per day.

The call has been followed with several cases of rapes and sexual assaults on women and girls in Syria who fall victim to extremist Al-Qaeda militants.

The insurgency in Syria which is going on with U.S.'s strong support is showing vicious incidents of human rights violations, almost all ignored by the western and regional allies of Washington.

The oil rich Sunni Arab states "Qatar, Saudi-Arabia and Kuwait etc, who've amass huge wealth from selling petroleum crude oil & gas, these oil rich countries are allegedly funding Islamist fundamentalist forces across the globe to promote radical Islamic studies and beliefs, for this purpose services of clerics is used in Islamic schools for indoctrinating the minds of people from Islamic communities with hatred and intolerance towards other religions. Young Sunni-Muslim men are taking up arms in hands rather than taking universities books in hands, and young Muslim girls being lured or being intimidated to participate in Sex-jihad. Young Sunni-Muslim girls having to surrender their dignity and bodies to relieve the Narcissistic Jihadist terrorist men by warming up these jihadists on bed.

The oil rich Sunni Arab states could well have or can easily make more productive use of their wealth to socially reform the Muslim community across the world, encourage the people of Muslim community to shed superstitions, and accept modern norms of contemporary world, so that the people of Muslim community can well integrate socially and culturally with people of other religions.

But, this world is a vicious circle, vicious society, the so-called super-power United States of America and its crony Britain, France and Germany to name a few, these western nations have brazenly bias foreign policies. They do not believe in practicing what they themselves preach, otherwise these western nations are big advocates of democracy, freedom of speech and all possible basic civil rights for common people, but, the realty is something else, U.S. and its allies say something in public but do the opposite of what they commit to people quite ostensibly in full public view.

U.S. and west-European nations like Britain, Germany, France accused the Russian President Vladimir Putin and his Government Administration of playing disruptive and destructive role in the internal political affairs of its neighbouring nation Ukraine, the western countries accusing the Russian government of aiding and supporting the separatist Rebel insurgent Militants inside Ukraine and working towards breaking Ukraine and harming Ukrainian's sovereignty and thereby Russia is causing disturbance to the peace and integrity of people of Ukraine. Hence the western countries like America, Germany,

Britain and France wasted No time in punishing the Russian government by imposing stiff and punitive economic sanction on the Russia in 2014.

Now that it is no big secret that since year 2011 the Islamic fundamentalist forces have made their intention clear that they want to take over countries like Syria, Iraq and Jordan and establish Islamic caliphate based on the principle of medieval era barbaric Islamic sharia law, hence when the Sunni-Muslim unrestrained terrorist elements like ISIS and Al Nusra unleashed terror inside Syria callously carrying out brutality against civilians in Syria and later in Iraq. So, **Mr Bashar al-Assad** being a president of Syria it was his constitutional obligation to fight against the brutal Sunni extremist forces to save citizens of his country. But, as Mr Assad being member of minority Shia community, but in stark contrast the friends and allies of western nations in Islamic countries are all belonging to Sunni-Muslim community, hence the western nations like Britain and France instead of helping secular and liberal president of Syria Mr Bashar Assad, the western nations governments having vested interest are/were hell bent on getting rid of a secular president of Syria like Mr Assad. The western nations tried to dislodge secular and liberal president like Mr Assad from power alleging that Syrian President is harming large section of Syrian population. USA, Britain and France openly trained and armed the Rebel Sunni Muslims elements, providing the so-called free Syrian army consisting of members of Sunni-Muslim community with training in combative army operations and also rendering sophisticated arms and ammunitions to the free Syrian army, who knows if or rather many reports openly suggests the same trained free Syrian army personnel and the ammunition provided by the western countries may have or rather really have joined ranks with terrorist groups like Al Nusra and ISIS, so it is allege that majority of jihadists in Al Qaeda and ISIS are the same folks whom the western countries have trained and provided weapons.

Therefore with regards to Israel's actions, whenever to defend its sovereignty and basic rights of its citizens, Israelis top priority is security for all its citizens hence defending their nation from so-called evil forces, the Israeli military and security forces whenever they feel security threat from fundamentalist Islamist militants like Palestine based "**Hamas**" whom Israel considers as terrorist group and threat for Israel, so, if Israel attacks the hideouts of the so-called Islamic terrorist group and in bargain ends up killing innocent civilians women and children, the western nations policy is to remain silent and ignorant and whenever asked their spokesperson standard reply will be that Israel has a fundamental right of defending itself therefore it is attacking the Sunni Islamist terrorist group, so for Israel or any other crony nations of western countries, or for that matter including America itself uses strong arm tactic in countries like Pakistan and Afghanistan as well in Yemen to curb terrorist activities American army hitting militant targets by flying unmanned Drone combat aircraft often Drone strikes misses targets and hits innocent civilians resulting in the deaths of innocents people. So, here, there is lot to desire about, that, the powerful nations like U.S. France and Germany have double standards one set of rule for themselves and for their friendly nations and opposite set of rules for nations that are not friendly and opposed to western nations.

I would like to point out something even western media has reporting it for long as it is observed by many politician and political analysts that the wealthy oil rich Arab nations like Qatar, Saudi Arabia, Kuwait are aggressively funding and aiding many of the fundamentalist Sunni Islamic jihadist terrorist groups all over the world, Islamic religious schools and institutions are perfect breeding ground for radicalizing young generation, Muslim children are brainwashed from early age and thought to profoundly oppose everything that is un-Islamic.

So when things are so crystal clear that majority populations (nearly 95%) of Sunni-Muslims have full sympathy for the Islamist jihadists because Sunni-Muslim brothers and sisters do not consider the jihadists (holy warrior) as terrorist, instead they justify the brutal activities of jihadi terrorist groups like Al Qaeda, Al Shabaab, and ISIS etc as religious holy duty and considers that the jihadists are the saviours Sunni Islam. Many surveys have found out that terrorist groups like Al Qaeda, ISIS, Boko-Haram overwhelmingly popular within their Sunni community and enjoys unprecedented support from Sunni-Muslim community.

Many intellectuals and political analysts ask few relevant questions, as to, why are the western nations not snapping and breaking economic and diplomatic relations with oil rich wealthy Arab countries like Qatar, Saudi Arabia and Kuwait? Why is another Sunni majority country Turkey still part of NATO alliance? On the contrary, what actually happens is that these western nations like America, Britain, France and Germany instead strengthens their relations firmly with the Sunni Arab nations, the same wealthy Arab nations who've been accused of funding the Islamic terrorist groups are being made the partners of western nations in their fight against the Radical Islamist jihadist organizations.

What a joke! How such an alliance be described? Same countries who are allegedly funding Sunni terrorists and the same Sunni terrorists army is/are targeting and killing Europeans and Americans, and these same Sunni nations are staunch western allies and partners in <u>war on terror</u>. Gosh this is ridiculous, what do you say? Funny, naïve, idiots or ugly; "have your own conclusion if any."

It is no secret again that in the 1980s, the Iraqi dictator Saddam Hussein was a blue eyed boy of America and its allies, when Saddam was helping the U.S. and European Corporates with lucrative business and arms deals. Also during the Russian led Soviet occupation of Afghanistan in the 1980s, it was none other than America's intelligence agency CIA helped in establishing the Taliban and Al Qaeda, in the 1980s U.S. use to call Al Qaeda's fighters and top commanders including Osama Bin Laden as moderates. U.S. intelligence agency CIA had propped up an alliance of Mujahideen of which Al Qaeda was principle constituent to fight against Russian led Soviet army inside Afghanistan. When it suits their purpose these western nations calls particular individuals or organizations as moderates and secular, otherwise those politicians or governments who opposes the western nation political policies or rub shoulders wrong way with western armies then U.S.A and its allies will try to defame unfriendly governments and politicians in some situation can also go to an extent of calling such governments supporters of terrorists. Because Saudis, Turkey and Israelis are allies of western countries hence all sins committed by them are ignored and find adequate reasons to justify brutalities, but countries such as "north-Korea, Iran or Syria" governments who are in opposite camp hence French, Britain and America detest these countries calls them terrorists.

In Political Arithmetic 2+2=5, Politics makes strange bedfellows, and many a time those bedfellows happens to be terrorist, yes, quite often and in many countries, Terrorism and politics goes hand in hand, both politicians and terrorists have to patronize each other for their survival.

It is always very important for all of us to study and to understand politics, most people are unconcern they say Politics is corrupt and boring and terrorism is wicked. "People around the World become Victim of Propaganda because they are NOT <u>Intellectually Competent,</u> as a result of which "Fools follows and obeys the Foolish" without applying their own mind and thoughts or verifying the facts.

Poor and Appalling "Analytical Skills" Foolish people "Believes or Disbelieves" anything and everything that is Shown or told to them without verifying facts or establishing the truth."

It concern us all, women in many parts of the world for many generations are dealing with very peculiar type of brutal cultural terrorism <u>FGM</u> or to say **"Female Genital Mutilation."**

Female genital mutilation (FGM), also known as female circumcision or female genital cutting, it is a destructive operation, during which the female genitals are partly or entirely removed or injured with the goals of inhibiting a woman's sexual feelings. Most often the mutilation is performed before puberty, often on girls between the age of four and eight, but recently it is increasingly performed on nurslings who are only a couple of days, weeks or months old.

History: "There is no secure information about the historical origin of the FGM, but apparently it started long time before the rising of Christianity and Islam. Originally, FGM is not related to any religion. It seems that early Roman and Arabic civilizations knew the practice which was linked to an ideal of virginity and chastity. These values are as we know very much cherished in the African and Arabic culture. Some historians believe that, In ancient Rome it was done to female slaves to oppress sexual activity and raise their value. Herodotus talks about an Egyptian women "genital" being cut, around 500 BC. Another theory says that it was performed by the Pharaohs to preserve their wives chastity during wartimes. A common name for the infibulation (But many historians are vary of the fact as in when, where and how did this "FGM" practice came into effect). The taboo about female sexuality and the related customs may be one of the reasons for the lack of historical information, as it is still presently the reason for the difficulty to get more precise data.

The historical roots lead to a combination of beliefs, superstition, cultural and social values than to religious reasons. FGM remains a mystery

It is estimated that approximately 100-140 million African women have undergone FGM worldwide and each year, a further 3 million girls are estimated to be at risk of the practice in Africa alone. Most of them live in African countries, a few in the Middle East and Asian countries, and increasingly in Europe, Australia, New Zealand, the United States of America and Canada.

Female genital mutilation (FGM) straddle national boundaries. FGM takes place in parts of the Middle East, i.e. in Yemen, Oman, Iraqi Kurdistan, amongst some Bedouin women in Israel, and was also practised by the Ethiopian Jews, and it is unclear whether they continue with the practice now that they are settled in Israel. FGM is also practised among Bohra Muslim populations in parts of India and Pakistan, and amongst Muslim populations in Malaysia and Indonesia.

During the 19th century in Europe, girls and women were cut to prevent masturbation and, related to it, mental diseases. Female homosexuality, nymphomania and hysteria were "cured" in this way.

Genital cutting is also commonplace in Egypt, with some 27.2 million women falling victim to it, the largest number in a single country in the world, according to Unicef figures.

The procedure is traditionally carried out by an older woman with no medical training. It is also performed by traditional midwives and occasionally by healers, barbers or nurses or doctors trained in Western medicine. Anaesthetics and antiseptic treatment are not generally used and the practice is usually carried out using basic tools such as knives, scissors, scalpels, pieces of glass and razor blades. Often iodine or a mixture of herbs is placed on the wound to tighten the vagina and stop the bleeding.

Pricking, piercing, cutting or stretching of the clitoris or the labia, also burning or scarring the genitals as well as ripping of the vaginal opening or the introduction of corrosive substances or herbs into the vagina in order to tighten it. Plus: any other procedure, which injures or circumcises the female genitalia. It reflects deep-rooted inequality between the sexes, and constitutes an extreme form of discrimination against women. It is nearly always carried out on minors and is a violation of the rights of children. The practice also violates a person's rights to health, security and physical integrity, the right to be free from torture and cruel, inhuman or degrading treatment, and the right to life when the procedure results in death.

Pairing is only possible because woman is not a monad, and has no sense of individuality, it is the endless striving of nothing to be something. It is thus that the duality of man and woman has gradually developed into complete dualism, to the dualism of the higher and lower lives, of subject and object, of form and matter, something and nothing. All metaphysical, all transcendental existence is logical and moral existence, woman is non-logical and non-moral. She has no dislike for what is logical and moral, she is not anti-logical, she is not anti-moral. She is not the negation, she is, rather, nothing. She is neither the affirmation nor the denial.

Article titled; **"Female Genital Cutting Fact Sheet"** describes about **FGC** in detail; "The terms female genital cutting (FGC), female circumcision, and female genital mutilation (FGM) all describe the cultural practice of partially or totally removing the external female genitalia. The minor form of FGC is when the clitoris is removed. The most severe form of FGC is when all external genitalia are removed and the vaginal opening is stitched nearly closed. Only a small opening is left for urine and menstrual blood.

All three terms describe the procedure that cuts away part or all of the external female genitalia. Deciding what exactly to call it is still being debated. Some people fear that parents may resent the implication that they are "mutilating" their daughters by participating in this largely cultural event, and so reject the term FGM in favour of FGC. Some people point out that the word "cutting" is less judgmental and relates better to terms used in many local languages. However, many women's health and human rights organizations use the word "mutilation" not only to describe the practice, but also to point out the violation of women's human rights.

FGC is performed on infants, girls, and women of all ages. The age at which girls are cut can vary widely from country to country, and even within countries. Most often, FGC happens before a girl reaches puberty. Sometimes, however, it is done just before marriage or during a woman's first pregnancy. In Egypt, about 90 percent of girls are cut between 5 and 14 years old. However, in Yemen, more than 75 percent of girls are cut before they are 2 weeks old. The average age at which a girl undergoes FGC is decreasing in some countries

(Burkina Faso, Côte d'Ivoire, Egypt, Kenya, and Mali). Researchers think it's possible that the average age of FGC is getting lower so that it can be more easily hidden from authorities in countries where there may be laws against it. It is also possible that FGC is performed on younger girls because they are less able to resist.

The practice of FGC is a cultural tradition performed across central Africa, in the southern Sahara, and in parts of the Middle East. Most women who have experienced FGC live in one of the 28 countries in Africa and the Middle East where FGC is practiced. Almost one-half of women who have experienced FGC live in Egypt or Ethiopia. (In Egypt, 2008 Demographic and Health Survey (DHS) information notes that female genital cutting rates are declining.)

To a lesser degree, FGC is practiced in Indonesia, Malaysia, Pakistan, and India. Some immigrants practice various forms of FGC in other parts of the world, including Australia, Canada, New Zealand, the United States, and in European nations.

Although many people believe that FGC is associated with Islam, it is not. FGC is not supported by any religion and is condemned by many religious leaders. The practice crosses religious barriers. Muslims, Christians, and Jews have been known to support FGC on their girls.

No religious text requires or even supports cutting female genitals. In fact, Islamic Shari'a protects children and protects their rights. From a Christian perspective, FGC has no religious grounds either. In fact, research shows that the relationship between religion and FGC is inconsistent at best.

However, even though religious texts don't support FGC, some people still think the two are linked and claim religious teachings support FGC. There are many reasons FGC is practiced, including social, economic, and political reasons. Those who support FGC believe that it will empower their daughters, ensure the girls get married, and protect the family's good name. In some groups, FGC is performed to show a girl's growth into womanhood and, as in the African "Masai community," marks the start of a girl's sexual debut."....

Basically, all social ills, like forced marriage, forced prostitutions, honour killings, female genital mutilation are such types of Social problems which operates like a revolving-door policy. As soon as one goes away, another turns up. For the most part, these problems are regarded as entirely separate from each other. Religion is a tool extensively used for generations by astute Religious hierarchy and Politicians to control the action and minds of great masses, religion holds back progress and development. Most if not all of these dedicated devout religious people are stereotypes and have a whimsical sense of humour.

It's a multi-dimensional battle women has to fight, what I mean is structural discrimination against female gender, Even in 21st century most countries governments have failed comprehensively in providing basic civic amenities like clean toilets, sanitation and clean water supply to every houses and to every citizens of their respective country. In most countries such as for example India, Pakistan, Bangladesh and many African countries there are millions of households where up to now they do not have basic facilities like good functional toilets and bathrooms also not available is regular clean water supply to their homes, and such infrastructure deficiency compels women to regularly travel long distances away from their homes to fetch water from wells, tube-wells, for their daily consumption, real hard work for these unfortunate women I must say, plus with no functional toilets and bathrooms which further exacerbate situation and adds more inconvenience because it makes life increasingly difficult for women to maintain high degree of hygiene, therefore impacting their health severely, women are then vulnerable to contracting various types of ailment and harmful diseases.

Women who do not keep themselves clean, be it during their periods or after masturbation or wearing improperly washed tight undergarments are at more risk. This leads to moistening of the vagina, and this moistness leads to the growth of bacteria and other parasites and thus, affecting the interiors and thus, causing itching, swelling, etc.

With regards to women's plight, as we dwell over and talk all about women's ordeal and agony, we need to assess the situation from ground level perspective to understand reasons behind women's excruciating pain with open mind and comprehensive practical and pragmatic thinking. We'll come to conclusion that most of the women's plight emanates from other women, covertly or overtly woman plays a crucial role in harming interest of another woman. The purpose for debate and discussions on complex human issues should be to know and to understand as in "<u>what is right</u>" and not "<u>who is right</u>," never be adamant to win debates.

It is not just my observation but many from elite class are also of the same opinion, that: **"women are woman's best friends and their worse foes,"** woman takes great lead in helping other women, but on the flip side it is a woman/women that shows no remorse whatsoever in ruining life of another woman, peers pressure or jealousy becomes prime reason and motive when a frustrated woman decides to systematically sabotage the life or good future prospects of other woman/women's, it so happens that many of the women expresses tremendous faith in another woman and discloses lots of their personal and family information, a woman most often thinks that trusting another woman would be her best option, hence woman frivolously trust a woman and discusses most of her personal matters which otherwise she should not, call them naïve or gullible, but when a woman trust fellow woman and seeks her good advice that's when many women invites unprecedented problems in their life.

No selfish man can ever succeed in his plan of seducing and exploiting a woman unless he has a support of a voracious crafty woman.

Some of those women whose own life is a failure and completely messed up, these unsuccessful and troubled women, when their life is in a disarray and has hit a bad patch, so, these women who are baffle and disgusted with the way their life's going thru, their thoughts allegedly are disturb, hence evil mind develop ulterior motives and their minds starts thinking this way, that, if my life is chaotic, if I and my family are unhappy, why should others be happy? Hence, why should other women thrive and be happy? that's when most women under frustration, adopts aggressive approach and starts to systematically harm others life by instigating them and provoking them to do all the wrong things, make all the wrong choices, which ultimately ruins the good future prospects of those unfortunate innocent people mainly women suffers the most, happy family lives are destroyed because of such nasty sly motives of supposedly our own friend or relatives.

There is a famous saying; "Behind every successful Man there is a Woman," I would just like to twist the famous saying, my own way, have a listen; "Behind the Pain and Agony of every Woman there is a woman."

Chapter 7

Women and girls throughout the world continue to experience violence, discrimination, inequality and poverty. Despite the existence of international covenants, regional treaties and domestic laws intended to codify and realise women's human rights, the reality is that women and girls are routinely unable to claim their basic rights.

The infamous "Bra Burning' Movement," in America in the 1960s is worth discussing, when it all started, the Females in the U.S. thought of a Novel way to start their struggle to gain equal rights. During 1960's women started protesting for equal rights. Women before 1960's were known as housewives and mothers and nothing but those two things. This aggravated many women and made them feel to reform this stereotype. The 1960's was the Time to do this. In the 1960's the "Bra Burning" was well known. Those "bra-burning days" can be traced to the boardwalk at Atlantic City, NJ, in "1968" when about 300 women's liberation demonstrators protested the Miss America pageant at the city's Convention Centre. People say that very few women actually burned their bras, but many supported those action. Women burned their bras because they felt that it proved a statement or made a stand for Women's rights. Another reason they burned their bras was because it was a symbol that showed wearing no bra at all. This was also meant to show independence of men. Many women thought that it meant freedom to be natural instead of pushed up. At the Miss American protest there were thrash-cans that women called freedom thrash-cans. Women threw things such as bras, girdles, curlers, tweezers, high-heels, etc, into them to be burned.

Many people might say that religiously sanctified subjugation of women, discrimination against women, and violence against women are things of the past. They are wrong! These things are alive and well today, and are becoming ever more common with the current increasing worldwide tendency towards religious fundamentalism based upon literal interpretations of the Bible and the Quran. Jews, Christians, and Muslims all berate women for causing humanity to be driven out of paradise. As a result of the original sin of the first woman, people lost the gift of immortality, had to work hard to find food, and were no longer blessed with the ability to interact directly with God.

What can I say about the tenuous status of women in religion that has not been written or documented extensively about? All of the major religions (Judaism, Christianity or Islam) have a bloody and violent history in their treatment of women. In fact, atheist and feminist prose emphasizes the concept of religion as a creation of MAN and not DIVINITY. This, in turn, makes religion a male invention, putting themselves in a position of power and subjugating women to forms of property and of a weaker frame of mind that requires male support and "guidance."

Women got there voting rights after men, but fairer sex empowerment notwithstanding and it capabilities not underestimated, they still have to get what they deserve. Come to think of it, some of us believe that the age of gender equality has arrived. But from many other perspectives, this still isn't true. One of the aspect, which leads some to believe this is a discrimination against women at workplace. The naysayers would vehemently deny that, but unfortunately, that is the harsh reality in quite a few parts of the globe in the so-called modern world.

In the Issues Affecting Women Programme, seek to contribute to a world in which women have the rights, capacity and opportunity to experience safety from violence and to enjoy their full and equal human rights. Specifically, the programme aims to build a strong and vibrant women's movement comprising of women who are empowered individually and collectively to challenge patriarchal norms, tackle the root causes of inequality and demand the full spectrum of their rights.

The forces that were holding back male wage growth were also acting on women's wages, but the gains made by women over this period in educational attainment, labour force attachment, and occupational upgrading, along with greater legal protections against discriminatory pay, initially compensated for adverse forces. In the last decade, however, women's wages have also dropped.

The pay divide between men and women has widened by another 80c an hour since the turn of the millennium. Women now earn an average $3.90 an hour less than men across all industries, down from an average $3.08 less in 2000, according to Weekend Herald calculations of Statistics New Zealand figures.

In every country where Women for Women International works, the food crisis is a life or death reality for the women we serve. For instance, the UN Food and Agriculture Organization has said that at least 18 million of Afghanistan's estimated 26.6 million people, mostly women and children, cannot meet their daily food and nutritional requirements.

Why might you need it? "Usually, the women are decent, hardworking, ethical and transparent workers. They are bewildered by conniving, self-serving, or nasty bitches and are likely to assume that somehow it is their fault. Perhaps they're imagining it; they aren't competent; they're too sensitive; they don't fit the role or place; or they wouldn't be heard if they spoke up," That's because Men don't want to know about it, and many people haven't realized the severity of its impact.

On a global scale, women cultivate more than half of all the food that is grown. In sub-Saharan Africa and the Caribbean, they produce up to 80 percent of basic foodstuffs. In Asia, they account for around 50 percent of food production. In Latin America, they are mainly engaged in subsistence farming, horticulture, poultry and raising small livestock." Yet women often get little recognition for that. In fact, many go unpaid. It is very difficult for these women to get the financial resources required to buy equipment etc, as many societies still do not accept, or realize, that there is a change in the "traditional" roles. Reasons for such disparity include the fact that women are generally underpaid and because they often perform low-status jobs, compared to men.

Abuses against women are relentless, systematic and widely tolerated, if not explicitly condoned. Violence and discrimination against women are global social epidemics.

Feminism has argued that women are as intrinsically worthwhile as men on the basis that there are no differences between men and women. Yet this is patently untrue. As it turns out, while the differences don't mean that women or men are better than one another, it is in these differences that the reasons for men's oppression of women can be found. Moreover, because women could not understand men's anger and selfishness, they tended to be actively intolerant of it.

Today the women's liberation movement is under attack as increasingly the media proclaims the end of feminism. Efforts to drive back women's rights, gained over the past twenty five years, gather momentum. Attacks on women's control over their fertility and their bodies, unequal wages, domestic violence and sexual abuse, lack of access to decent jobs and continued discriminatory practices are all part of what has been termed the ``backlash'' against the women's movement.

Feminists themselves are divided about which way to proceed-whether to go on the offensive, or simply defend the gains of the past-or even to sacrifice the needs of the great majority of women in order to preserve gains for a privileged few.

It has been linked to stereotypes and gender roles, and may include the belief that one sex or gender is intrinsically superior to another. Sexism affects both men and women but primarily it's women who suffers most. Explicitly speaking, Sexism is an offensive reminder of the way cultures perceive and treats women. Extreme sexism may foster sexual harassment, rape and other forms and types of sexual violence.

Rising inequality and ever so growing income gap between the rich and poor, almost half of the world's wealth is now owned by just one percent of the population, Massive concentration of economic resources in the hands of fewer people presents a significant threat to inclusive political and economic systems. Instead of moving forward together, people are increasingly separated by economic and political power, inevitably heightening social tensions and increasing the risk of civil society breakdown.

Bi-polar division between privilege-class and under-class also have its implication on civil society, because ever so growing gap between Rich and Poor causes civil unrest, sharp economic inequality creates many social problems.

Tremendous breakthrough achieved in advancement of science and technology, but 21st century tech-revolution unfortunately isn't creating enough new jobs or business opportunities, in fact <u>Advance technology</u> artificial intelligence and robotic tech-machines is/are apparently destroying jobs and business opportunities and it is evident that over the past couple of decades upgradation of technology hence companies relying more on machines to do work both in factories and in offices which has made many highly qualified and skilled workforce redundant, therefore compelling many of the highly qualified <u>Master-Degree</u> and diploma holders and professionals to take and accept low paying sub-standard jobs, like serving Pizza & Coffee in Restaurants or driving Taxi, working at gas station or doing odd jobs like office assistant etc.

Many recent college graduates are currently unemployed. They contend that there are very few jobs comparable to their education. There are some recent college graduates who remain unemployed 4 years after their graduation. They maintain that they rather be unemployed than to take a job which is educationally beneath them which they contend would seriously derail their career plans. They want jobs which would guarantee some semblance of a middle income lifestyle. However, these jobs are becoming few and far between. While there are some recent college graduates who take these sub-standard "Mcjobs" and work on them until they could do better.

The reason graduates do not get jobs is not because they lack the hard (technical) skills, but because they are deficient in the really hard (used to be called soft) skills, such as the capacity for self-expression. You can accumulate as many degrees as you wish, but unless you come as the full package, you will remain unemployed.

The quality a person needs in him/her is to display confidence. Not false confidence, that smooth- talking gibberish you hear at political rallies. Real confidence means looking someone in the eye when speaking, or confidently gripping the hand of a client during greeting, or taking the lead in a conversation when everybody else seems to be floundering.

There are hundred reasons to do things you want to do in life and hundred reasons not to do things that you want to do, it all depends what option you select.

Fickle minded person, are people with such a characteristic, *they don't know what they want in life*, hesitation and full of confusion, such people not only do they disrupt their own progress, but they also harm and halt progress of others as well, and always a spoilsport will ruin other people's peace. In stark contrast a person who has **self-confidence** and strong **body-language** will always attract attention of people wherever he/she goes, people in our society always like, respect, believe and trust a person who is self-confident, experts are of the opinion that self-confidence is first step towards Progress and development so as to achieve success in life.

To eradicate poverty there is a need to provide each person of working-age a job, worldwide in every city, town and villages there is need to have better healthcare facilities and special provision needs to be made to provide monetary help and assistance to elders and senior citizens. Too much talk but very little action, politicians and also elite class expresses concern and discusses ideas to eradicate poverty, but there apparently is no tangible action plan ready and there is no one actually ready to honestly work to help get rid of poverty, politicians and businessmen make big promises but under-delivers on their promises.

Female gender particularly vulnerable, because women have failed to break through gender barrier in the area of negotiations, even in female dominated fields it has been observed that women don't have advantage, they fail to recognize diverse strategies that women desires to become. Anxiety manifest itself in different ways and situations, one of which is at workplace, Women takes time out for "*family time*" while men takes time out to "*change career*" which apparently have "serious implications.

Have a perspective challenge your perspective that will help you make right decisions.

We all have expectations in our lives, what we want out of life and what we want to become in life, managing our expectations, the problem arise in a person's life when their expectations do not materialize, most people especially educated folks goof up bigtime in life, because they are unaware of basic ground realities. Schools and universities text books makes a person book-smart what counts more in real life is to be **street-smart**.

What people need to have the most? It is to have a quality **"Analytical Skills,"** to solve complex and uncomplicated problems.

No matter how good an orator you are, how good is your communication skills and proficiency in language/languages you may have. But, what actually will save you from many troubles of life is a **Good Listening Skills**, yes, most people invites unnecessary troubles in their life as well as many family's disintegrate because of **Bad Listening Skills**. **Good Listening Skills** is a Master's Art, unfortunately most don't know the great significance of **Listening Skills.**

The most important kind of freedom is to be what you really are. You trade in your reality for a rate. You trade in your sense for an act. You give up your ability to feel, and in exchange, put on a mask. There can't be any large-scale revolution, on an individual level. It's got to happen inside first.

All emotions are about perception of bondage, from complete connection with you-really-are too severely pinching yourself off from who-you-really-are, which do you want more of?

Everything in life is temporary, so if things are going "Good" enjoy it because good things are not going to last forever, if things are "Bad" don't worry as bad things won't last forever.

Have a assertive and positive approach toward life, differences and contentious issues needs to be sorted out amicably through dialogue and cordial discussions, one very important lesson to learn in life is, never to **Argue**, *Argument is worse form of violence*; arguments normally have devastating consequences, arguments destroys personal image and gives bad reputation, arguments strains relationships or even causes breakup of relationships, be it in personal life, professional or business life, always avoid arguments.

www.ingramcontent.com/pod-product-compliance
Lightning Source LLC
Chambersburg PA
CBHW062016280526
45787CB00005B/2118